MESILA
Providing The Path to Financial Stability

MESILA JUNIOR HIGH SCHOOL PROGRAM

Teacher's Guide

Sephardic Yeshiva Version

Teacher's Guide - Sephardic Yeshiva Version

ISBN 978-1-941902-31-8

Please note:

This material is intended for use exclusively in the context of a Mesila-authorized course. It may not be used without prior written permission from Mesila's Jerusalem headquarters.

MESILA
Providing The Path to Financial Stability

Questions or comments may be sent to:

Mesila

P.O.B. 57116 Jerusalem 9157002, Israel
Tel: +972.2.500.0475 • Fax: +972.2.500.0478
info@mesila.org • www.mesila.org
Reg. Amuta No. 580361236

Mesila USA

POB 838 Monsey NY 10952
Tel: 212.784.6780
info@mesilausa.org
www.mesilausa.org

Mesila UK

Tel: 333 344 1711
info@mesilauk.org • www.mesilauk.org
Reg. Charity No. 1114573

Table of Contents

Dear Educator,

Mesila is proud to introduce the most recent addition to our educational series: the Junior High School program, aimed at grades 6-8. Mesila's mission is to help people achieve financial stability, and we have found that prevention is the most effective strategy is combating financial difficulties.

In today's dizzying world of credit cards, advertising, and consumerism, kids are bombarded from the youngest age with harmful, anti-Torah messages that encourage them to buy, buy, buy, and to spend now, pay later. Even the most upstanding Torah publications are full of ads urging people to indulge because they "deserve" it, and no schoolyard is immune to conversations about designer clothing, gourmet nosh, and extravagant vacations. These conversations are far from innocent, since they create crushing social pressure and unfair expectations of parents.

Whether we like it or not, our children use money, think about money, and talk about money much more than kids did in previous generations. Considering these frightening realities, it's never too early to start inculcating kids with healthy, Torah based financial attitudes such as controlled consumption, sensitivity to others, integrity, delayed gratification, avoiding dependence, etc.

We welcome suggestions, questions, and other feedback.
Feel free to contact us at info@mesila.org or (212) 784 6780
(9 a.m. – 3 p.m. EST; please leave a message).

Mrs. B. Weinberg **Mrs. M. Heimowitz**

Curriculum Development, Mesila

UNIT 1

Introduction: CRASH COURSE IN ECONOMICS

Unit 1

Introduction: Crash Course in Economics

1. *To convey basic economic terms and concepts.*
2. *To understand what money is and what gives it value.*
3. *To learn that money is a tool that can lead us towards a higher purpose.*
4. *To discover how the flow of money contributes to the health of the economy.*
5. *To learn that chessed forms the underpinning of the world and its economic realities.*
6. *To appreciate the concept that true wealth is a function of being happy with what you have.*

Materials

- 1 lesson plan for teacher
- Workbook pages:
  - What is Money?
  - Follow the Trail of the $50 Bill
  - The Value of Money

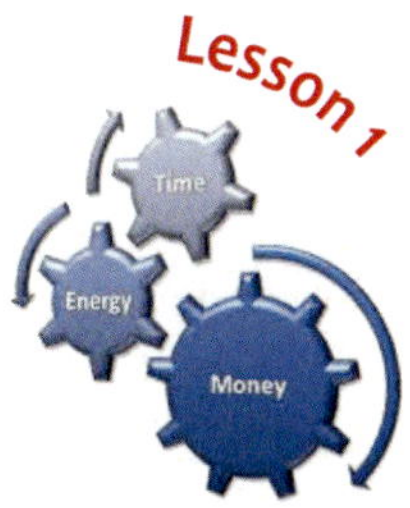

What is Money?

Let's put money in its place.

The very concept of money triggers deep-seated emotional reactions in people, both adults and children. Money is mistakenly seen both as an all-powerful answer to all problems, and as the root of all evil. Money receives so much attention, yet is so misunderstood.

What is the truth? How does the Torah view money?

In the Torah view, money is merely a tool, a means to an end. Just as we have been given tools such as hammers, scissors, and knives that can both build and destroy, or hands, feet, and a mouth that can be used for positive or negative purposes, the money at our disposal can also be used in a way that is beneficial or detrimental. Our challenge as Jews is to take the money that Hashem has given us and use it for a higher purpose, namely, *avodat Hashem.*

Any discussion of money in a Jewish classroom, and certainly a course that revolves around finance, must repeatedly emphasize the proper place of money in Torah hashkafah. Our job as educators is to strip money of its emotional overtones, and train our students to relate to money for what it is: a tool, and nothing else.

We have to convey that in the Torah value system, **money is:**

- NOT the marker of success
- NOT the cause of happiness
- NOT a goal in and of itself
- NOT an entitlement
- NOT all-important

Money IS:

- Necessary for healthy functioning
- A gift that brings with it the responsibility to help others
- A powerful tool that has to be controlled and used carefully
- A means of achieving higher goals

Before presenting the concepts in the lessons that follow, or in the course of the presentation, you may want to engage your students in a discussion of the proper place of money in the Jewish value system. One way of doing this is through an associations activity, where they write down or call out their automatic mental response to the word "money," or other trigger words, such as happiness, tzedakah, or saving. You may be surprised to hear their associations.

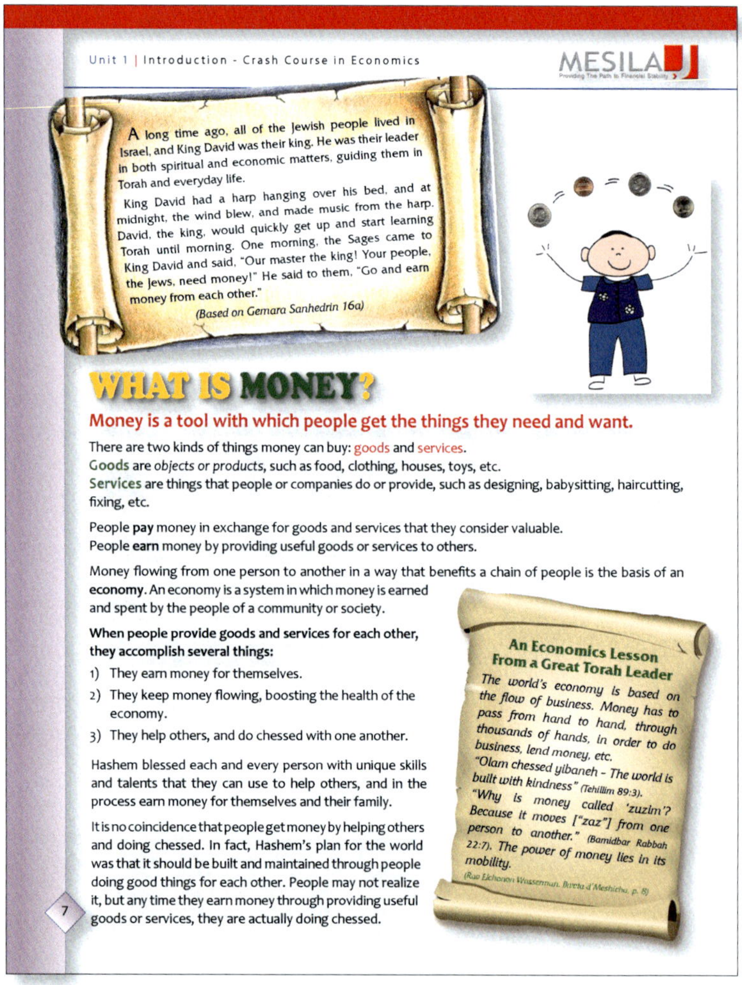

A long time ago, all of the Jewish people lived in Israel, and King David was their king. He was their leader in both spiritual and economic matters, guiding them in Torah and everyday life.

King David had a harp hanging over his bed, and at midnight, the wind blew, and made music from the harp. David, the king, would quickly get up and start learning Torah until morning. One morning, the Sages came to King David and said, "Our master the king! Your people, the Jews, need money!" He said to them, "Go and earn money from each other."

(Based on Gemara Sanhedrin 16a)

WHAT IS MONEY?

Money is a tool with which people get the things they need and want.

There are two kinds of things money can buy: goods and services.
Goods are *objects or products*, such as food, clothing, houses, toys, etc.
Services are things that people or companies do or provide, such as designing, babysitting, haircutting, fixing, etc.

People **pay** money in exchange for goods and services that they consider valuable.
People **earn** money by providing useful goods or services to others.

Money flowing from one person to another in a way that benefits a chain of people is the basis of an **economy**. An economy is a system in which money is earned and spent by the people of a community or society.

When people provide goods and services for each other, they accomplish several things:

1) They earn money for themselves.
2) They keep money flowing, boosting the health of the economy.
3) They help others, and do chessed with one another.

Hashem blessed each and every person with unique skills and talents that they can use to help others, and in the process earn money for themselves and their family.

It is no coincidence that people get money by helping others and doing chessed. In fact, Hashem's plan for the world was that it should be built and maintained through people doing good things for each other. People may not realize it, but any time they earn money through providing useful goods or services, they are actually doing chessed.

An Economics Lesson From a Great Torah Leader

The world's economy is based on the flow of business. Money has to pass from hand to hand, through thousands of hands, in order to do business, lend money, etc.

"Olam chessed yibaneh – The world is built with kindness" (Tehillim 89:3).

"Why is money called 'zuzim'? Because it moves ["zaz"] from one person to another." (Bamidbar Rabbah 22:7). The power of money lies in its mobility.

(Rav Elchonon Wasserman, Ikveta d'Meshicha, p. 8)

Workbook: What is Money?

Goal

To understand how the movement of money is the basis of economic activity and prosperity.

Workbook: Follow the Trail of the $50 Bill

To the teacher

In this worksheet, we follow the trail of a $50 bill and show how much economic benefit accrues along this journey. Another idea that can be developed from this tale is the value of initiative. How many people just sit back and wait passively for solutions to materialize, when they themselves hold the keys to making those solutions happen? This is true in all realms: economic, social, medical, even spiritual.

You may decide to use this tale as a springboard for a discussion of the concept of being proactive rather than reactive or passive.

The concept of initiative will be developed further in Unit 2: Money in Action.

Workbook: Follow the Trail of the $50 Bill / Review

Unit 1 | Introduction - Crash Course in Economics

MESILA

Follow the Trail of the $50 Bill

Here's an example of how the flow of money from one hand to another strengthens the economy while helping people at the same time:

A Microeconomic Tale

Gabriel Levi, age 10, really wants his own etrog, and he has an idea of how he can buy his own set: He has an aravot bush in his backyard, and he'll sell aravot outside the synagogue before Succot and use the money to buy the etrog. His mother gives him permission to cut branches from the bush and sell them, and he sells the aravot for $5 a pair. He sells 10 pairs, and earns $50. He puts the $50 bill in his wallet and goes to spend the money on his very own etrog.

Mr. Harari is an etrog dealer. One day before Succot, Gabriel Levi walks into his shop. "I have $50 to spend on an etrog," he says proudly. "Can you show me the nicest etrog you have for that price?"

Mr. Harari helps Gabriel choose a lovely etrog, and places the $50 in his wallet.

Erev Succot, Mrs. Harari looks at her watch and sees that it's already 10:30 in the morning. "Uh oh," she thinks, "my succah still has no lights!" Mr. Harari is still out selling etrogim, and Mrs. Harari doesn't know what to do. She quickly picks up the phone and calls Chaim, the electrician. "Can you come down and set up the lights in my succah?" she pleads.

"Sure," Chaim says. "I'll be right over."

An hour later, the Hararis' succah is bright and cheery, and Mrs. Harari is bright and cheery as well as she pulls out the $50 to pay Chaim.

The $50 safely in his pocket, Chaim the electrician runs over to Levi's Liquor Store just before closing time and buys wine for the Chag. "Great," he thinks. "I was running low on cash, and I didn't know if I'd be able to get the wine I wanted for simchat Chag."

Mr. Levi closes his liquor store and goes home to get ready for the Chag. "Gabriel," he calls, "did you end up buying yourself an etrog?"

"Yes, Abba," Gabriel says excitedly. "Look! Isn't it beautiful?"

"It sure is," says Mr. Levi. "How much was it?"

"Fifty dollars," says Gabriel. "That's what I made selling aravot."

Mr. Levi reaches into his pocket. "I just made one last extra sale as I was closing the store," he says, "and it was exactly $50. Here – I want to pay for your etrog."

The End

8

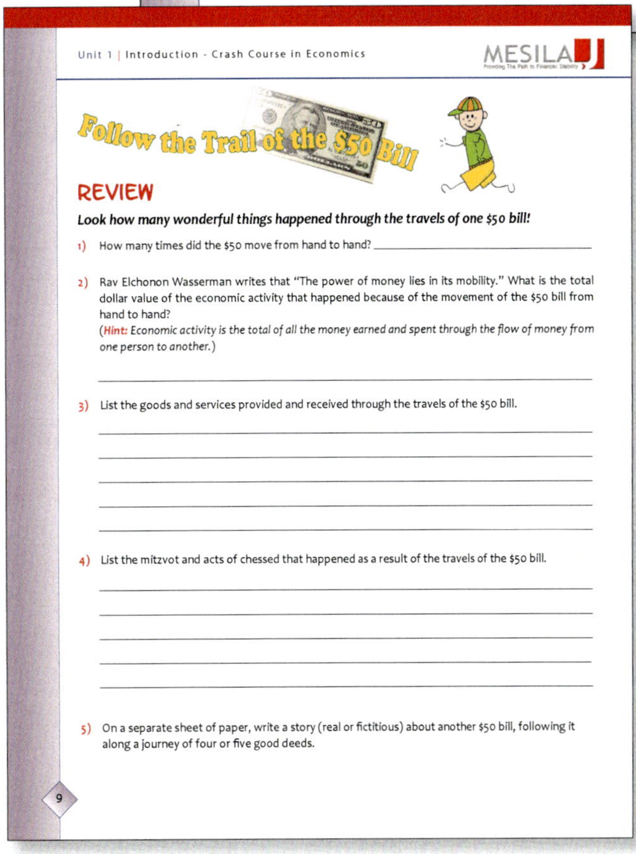

Unit 1 | Introduction - Crash Course in Economics

MESILA

Follow the Trail of the $50 Bill

REVIEW

Look how many wonderful things happened through the travels of one $50 bill!

1) How many times did the $50 move from hand to hand? ____________

2) Rav Elchonon Wasserman writes that "The power of money lies in its mobility." What is the total dollar value of the economic activity that happened because of the movement of the $50 bill from hand to hand?
(*Hint: Economic activity is the total of all the money earned and spent through the flow of money from one person to another.*)

____

3) List the goods and services provided and received through the travels of the $50 bill.

____

4) List the mitzvot and acts of chessed that happened as a result of the travels of the $50 bill.

____

5) On a separate sheet of paper, write a story (real or fictitious) about another $50 bill, following it along a journey of four or five good deeds.

9

Workbook: The Value of Money

Goal

To demonstrate the limitations of money's worth.

A. Putting Money in Perspective

In the following worksheet, we present the idea that money has no intrinsic worth. What gives money value is the fact that people trust and accept the currency.

The purpose of conveying this message about money is, once again, to put money in perspective. Yes, we need money, and yes, money is important, but not for its own sake – only for what can be done with it. If money has no intrinsic worth, then there is no sense in pursuing it as an end in and of itself, nor is there a reason to obsess or become consumed with it.

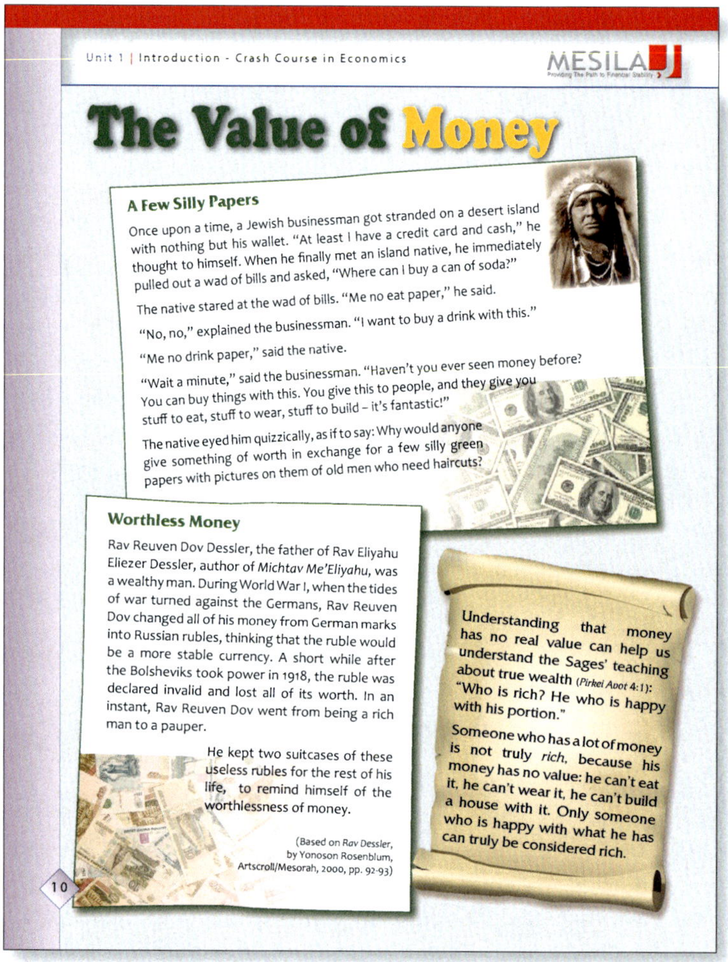
Unit 1 | Introduction - Crash Course in Economics

The Value of Money

A Few Silly Papers

Once upon a time, a Jewish businessman got stranded on a desert island with nothing but his wallet. "At least I have a credit card and cash," he thought to himself. When he finally met an island native, he immediately pulled out a wad of bills and asked, "Where can I buy a can of soda?"

The native stared at the wad of bills. "Me no eat paper," he said.

"No, no," explained the businessman. "I want to buy a drink with this."

"Me no drink paper," said the native.

"Wait a minute," said the businessman. "Haven't you ever seen money before? You can buy things with this. You give this to people, and they give you stuff to eat, stuff to wear, stuff to build – it's fantastic!"

The native eyed him quizzically, as if to say: Why would anyone give something of worth in exchange for a few silly green papers with pictures on them of old men who need haircuts?

Worthless Money

Rav Reuven Dov Dessler, the father of Rav Eliyahu Eliezer Dessler, author of *Michtav Me'Eliyahu*, was a wealthy man. During World War I, when the tides of war turned against the Germans, Rav Reuven Dov changed all of his money from German marks into Russian rubles, thinking that the ruble would be a more stable currency. A short while after the Bolsheviks took power in 1918, the ruble was declared invalid and lost all of its worth. In an instant, Rav Reuven Dov went from being a rich man to a pauper.

He kept two suitcases of these useless rubles for the rest of his life, to remind himself of the worthlessness of money.

(Based on *Rav Dessler*, by Yonoson Rosenblum, Artscroll/Mesorah, 2000, pp. 92-93)

Understanding that money has no real value can help us understand the Sages' teaching about true wealth (*Pirkei Avot* 4:1): "Who is rich? He who is happy with his portion."

Someone who has a lot of money is not truly *rich*, because his money has no value: he can't eat it, he can't wear it, he can't build a house with it. Only someone who is happy with what he has can truly be considered rich.

10

However, our goal is not to dismiss money as worthless or irrelevant. Our Sages teach that righteous people value their money more than their very selves (Chullin 91a), and the reason they value their money is because they understand that it is a gift from Hashem that is meant to be used to fulfill their mission in this world.

Therefore, money has to be taken seriously and treated responsibly. We will expand on this idea in Unit 7, Respecting Property.

B. What is Money Really Worth?

Question: Why does money have value?

Answer: Because people in a society accept it as payment.

Background

In ancient times, precious metals such as gold and silver, were used as money, or **currency**. Alternatively, people traded goods or services to get what they needed. (This was called **barter**.)

In modern times, paper money is standard currency. Unlike gold and silver, unlike valuable items that can be bartered, paper money has no real value other than the paper it's printed on. The only reason that money has value is because people accept it as payment. The only reason that people accept it as payment is because they think it has value.

Question: What would happen if people suddenly stopped thinking that money has value?

Answer: Money would have no value. This has happened in many different countries in modern times.

Example: Israel suffered terrible **inflation** and **currency devaluation** in the 1970s and 1980s. (You may want to introduce these concepts to your class more in-depth.) In 1985, the old Israeli shekel was replaced with the New Israeli Shekel (NIS) – at a rate of 1,000 old shekels to one new shekel! This was after the lira, or Israeli pound, was replaced in 1980 with the shekel.

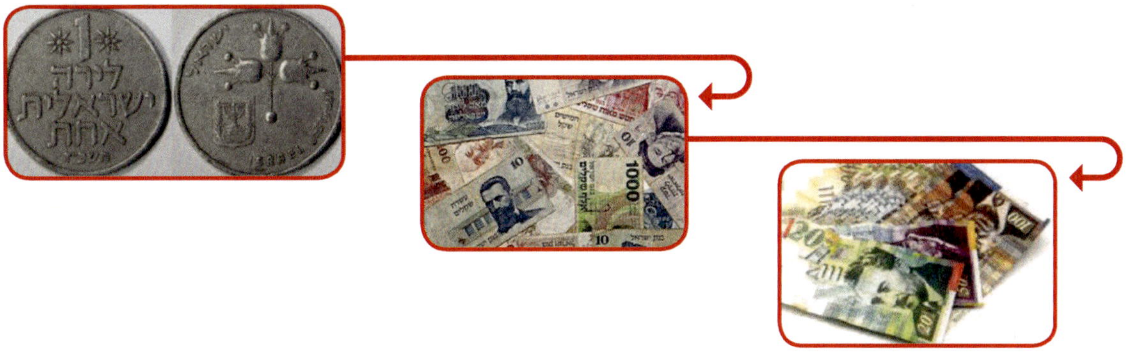

C. Who is Truly Wealthy?

At the end of worksheet #2, we briefly introduce what is perhaps *the* most central principle of finance in Jewish thought. While we are all familiar with the concept of "Who is rich? He who is happy with his portion," we tend to understand it as an ethical teaching, rather than as a statement of economic reality. But if money has no intrinsic worth, then how can someone be rich, even if the financial sense, just by owning a lot of it?

Furthermore, it's patently obvious that wealth is entirely subjective. A tribal chief living in a large mud hut in Africa will feel wealthy compared to his subjects living in smaller mud huts, whereas a person living in the largest hut in America would feel poverty-stricken. (We will discuss this idea further in Unit 4: Needs & Wants.) On the other hand, Baron Rothschild felt rich without running water or a refrigerator. Can anyone today say the same?

Therefore, whether or not a person is wealthy depends entirely on whether he feels wealthy. Who is richer? A billionaire who is dissatisfied with his life and oblivious to his good fortune? Or a teenager who just earned her first summer job paycheck and is delighted with her earnings?

Feeling wealthy has much less to do with the amount of money you have in the bank, and much more to do with how you feel about what you have. "Who is rich? He who is happy with his portion."

MESILA
Providing The Path to Financial Stability

UNIT 2

MONEY IN ACTION

Unit 2

Money in Action

1. *To explore different payment methods and evaluate their advantages and drawbacks.*
2. *To examine positive and negative reactions to financial shortfalls.*
3. *To internalize the value of being a giver or lender, and the distastefulness of being a taker or a borrower.*
4. *To identify hidden loans (i.e., credit cards and installment plans).*
5. *To emphasize the value of saving and understand that saving is a loan to yourself.*
6. *To highlight the benefits of initiative.*
7. *To recognize the steps of building a basic business plan, in both the business and non-profit contexts.*
8. *To reinforce the centrality of tzedakah in Jewish life.*

Materials

- 2 lesson plans
- Workbook pages:
  - Money's Many Identities
  - Financial Shortfalls: What Happens When You Run Out of Money
  - Simon Says
  - Pat's Plans
- 1 assignment/class activity: Class Tzedakah Campaign

Lesson 1: Money Management

To the teacher:

In this lesson, we will focus on two distinct aspects of money management: payment methods and handling financial shortfalls.

We examine three primary methods of payment: cash, checks, and credit cards. These are presented first in riddle form, with a follow-up activity that highlights the unique features of each method and asks the students to identify which method corresponds to which description.

No payment method is "good" or "bad" – each has its benefits and drawbacks. However, the dangers of credit cards should be emphasized, in light of the fact that so many people have fallen into the trap of irresponsible credit card use. You may also choose to discuss the workings of credit cards in more detail. (Mesila can provide you with supplementary material on this topic.)

Workbook:
Money's Many Identities

Goal

To introduce various methods of payment and assess the pros and cons of using cash, checks, and credit cards.

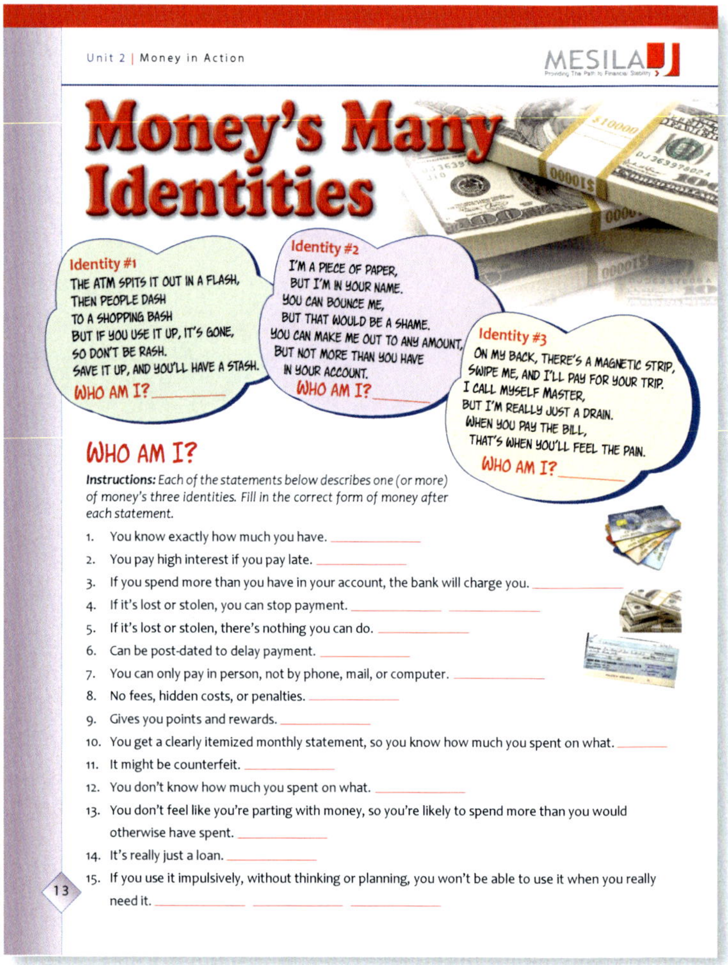
Unit 2 | Money in Action

Money's Many Identities

Identity #1
THE ATM SPITS IT OUT IN A FLASH,
THEN PEOPLE DASH
TO A SHOPPING BASH
BUT IF YOU USE IT UP, IT'S GONE,
SO DON'T BE RASH.
SAVE IT UP, AND YOU'LL HAVE A STASH.
WHO AM I? ________

Identity #2
I'M A PIECE OF PAPER,
BUT I'M IN YOUR NAME.
YOU CAN BOUNCE ME,
BUT THAT WOULD BE A SHAME.
YOU CAN MAKE ME OUT TO ANY AMOUNT,
BUT NOT MORE THAN YOU HAVE
IN YOUR ACCOUNT.
WHO AM I? ________

Identity #3
ON MY BACK, THERE'S A MAGNETIC STRIP,
SWIPE ME, AND I'LL PAY FOR YOUR TRIP.
I CALL MYSELF MASTER,
BUT I'M REALLY JUST A DRAIN.
WHEN YOU PAY THE BILL,
THAT'S WHEN YOU'LL FEEL THE PAIN.
WHO AM I? ________

WHO AM I?

Instructions: *Each of the statements below describes one (or more) of money's three identities. Fill in the correct form of money after each statement.*

1. You know exactly how much you have. ________
2. You pay high interest if you pay late. ________
3. If you spend more than you have in your account, the bank will charge you. ________
4. If it's lost or stolen, you can stop payment. ________ ________
5. If it's lost or stolen, there's nothing you can do. ________
6. Can be post-dated to delay payment. ________
7. You can only pay in person, not by phone, mail, or computer. ________
8. No fees, hidden costs, or penalties. ________
9. Gives you points and rewards. ________
10. You get a clearly itemized monthly statement, so you know how much you spent on what. ________
11. It might be counterfeit. ________
12. You don't know how much you spent on what. ________
13. You don't feel like you're parting with money, so you're likely to spend more than you would otherwise have spent. ________
14. It's really just a loan. ________
15. If you use it impulsively, without thinking or planning, you won't be able to use it when you really need it. ________ ________ ________

13

Running out of money can be an extremely embarrassing and stressful experience, for both adults and children. It is important, however, to differentiate between true poverty and simple cash-flow snags. An occasional lack of funds does not mean that a person is poor – in fact, there are billionaires who run out of cash. A chronic shortage of money is a truer indication of a serious financial problem. It should be noted, however, that even serious financial problems are often the result of mismanagement, not deprivation.

Children do not – and should not – see the bigger picture of their family finances, and therefore, if they sense that their parents are low on money, they may become frightened and anxious. The lack the maturity to understand that just because their mother can't buy them shoes today, or their father is scrounging to pay the grocery bill, that does not mean that they are destitute or in imminent danger of being evicted from their home.

In the handout that follows, one of our aims is to reassure students that occasional financial shortfalls are normal, and that everyone experiences ups and downs when it comes to their money. Part of having a healthy attitude to money is being able to weather some financial stress without panic or hysteria.

People who are able to weather financial stress calmly are less likely to fall into the traps of borrowing and dependency. In addition, they are more pleasant to be around, for their overall functioning is not controlled by the vicissitudes of their finances. Financial stress causes or contributes to so many different types of problems: shalom bayis, kids at risk, psychological and physical health, etc. By giving children the tools to maintain their equilibrium in the face of common financial challenges, we will be giving them an invaluable gift for life.

Workbook: Financial Shortfalls

WHAT HAPPENS WHEN YOU RUN OUT OF MONEY?

Goal: To describe the different possible reactions to financial shortfalls.

In the workbook pages that follow, we repeatedly refer to a cast of characters consisting of Sandy Schnorrer, Barry Borrower, Pat Planner, Calvin Coper, and Scott Saver. These five characters represent five different approaches to dealing with financial challenges – two of which are negative, and three of which are positive. Rather than lecture the students about healthy and unhealthy financial habits, we have chosen to portray these habits in action by creating caricatures who role-play each of the possible habits.

We deliberately chose non-Jewish names for these characters, to avoid any scenario in which a kid in the class happened to have the same name as one of the characters. (Imagine if we had called the kid Shalom Schnorrer and there was a kid named Shalom in the class…)

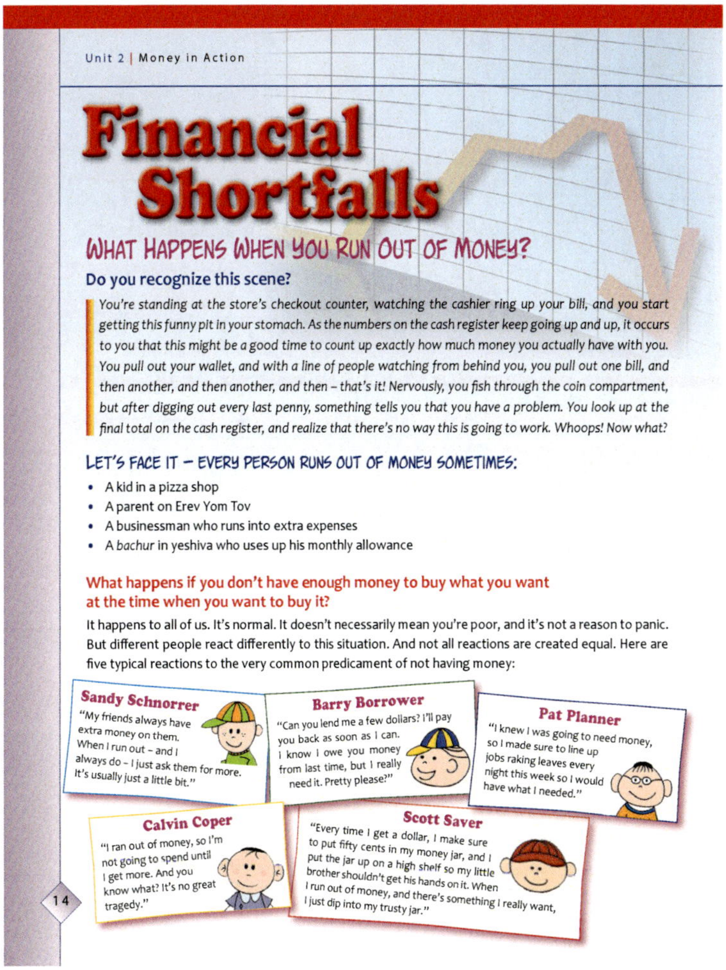

Unit 2 | Money in Action

Financial Shortfalls

WHAT HAPPENS WHEN YOU RUN OUT OF MONEY?

Do you recognize this scene?

You're standing at the store's checkout counter, watching the cashier ring up your bill, and you start getting this funny pit in your stomach. As the numbers on the cash register keep going up and up, it occurs to you that this might be a good time to count up exactly how much money you actually have with you. You pull out your wallet, and with a line of people watching from behind you, you pull out one bill, and then another, and then another, and then – that's it! Nervously, you fish through the coin compartment, but after digging out every last penny, something tells you that you have a problem. You look up at the final total on the cash register, and realize that there's no way this is going to work. Whoops! Now what?

LET'S FACE IT – EVERY PERSON RUNS OUT OF MONEY SOMETIMES:

- A kid in a pizza shop
- A parent on Erev Yom Tov
- A businessman who runs into extra expenses
- A *bachur* in yeshiva who uses up his monthly allowance

What happens if you don't have enough money to buy what you want at the time when you want to buy it?

It happens to all of us. It's normal. It doesn't necessarily mean you're poor, and it's not a reason to panic. But different people react differently to this situation. And not all reactions are created equal. Here are five typical reactions to the very common predicament of not having money:

Sandy Schnorrer
"My friends always have extra money on them. When I run out – and I always do – I just ask them for more. It's usually just a little bit."

Barry Borrower
"Can you lend me a few dollars? I'll pay you back as soon as I can. I know I owe you money from last time, but I really need it. Pretty please?"

Pat Planner
"I knew I was going to need money, so I made sure to line up jobs raking leaves every night this week so I would have what I needed."

Calvin Coper
"I ran out of money, so I'm not going to spend until I get more. And you know what? It's no great tragedy."

Scott Saver
"Every time I get a dollar, I make sure to put fifty cents in my money jar, and I put the jar up on a high shelf so my little brother shouldn't get his hands on it. When I run out of money, and there's something I really want, I just dip into my trusty jar."

14

Workbook: Discussion Questions

Note: These questions and the concepts they contain are an integral part of the handout.

1. Which of the above reactions are positive, and which are negative?
2. Everyone's different. Of the three positive reactions above, which do you feel is most suited to your personality?
3. There's a mitzvah to give tzedakah. There's a mitzvah to give someone a loan. But what about taking tzedakah or taking a loan? That's NOT a mitzvah. In fact, in Birkat HaMazon, we ask Hashem that we not be needy of people's gifts or loans.
   a. Which of the above characters are the recipients of other people's gifts and loans?
   b. Which of the above characters are in a position to give and lend money to others?
   c. What advice would you give someone to help him turn himself from a taker or borrower into a giver?
   d. What advice would you give to someone who has trouble giving or lending his money or possessions?

Lesson 2:
Good Financial Habits – Savings & Initiative

In the previous lesson, we introduced the different identities of money – cash, check, credit card – and presented a variety of reactions, positive and negative, to financial shortfalls. We discussed the idea that borrowing and dependency are problematic and distasteful, and we expand on this idea in the following lesson by contrasting healthy financial habits with unhealthy ones and stressing the positive ways of coping with minor financial challenges.

Workbook: Simon Says

Goal

To contrast healthy and unhealthy financial habits.

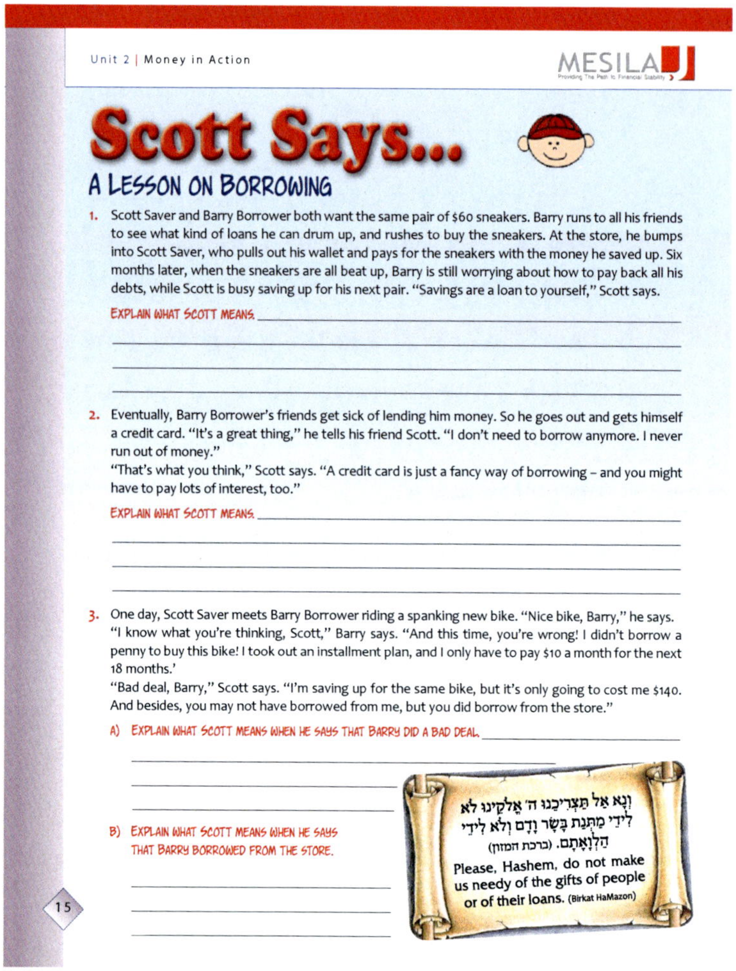
Unit 2 | Money in Action
MESILA
Providing The Path to Financial Stability

Scott Says...

A LESSON ON BORROWING

1. Scott Saver and Barry Borrower both want the same pair of $60 sneakers. Barry runs to all his friends to see what kind of loans he can drum up, and rushes to buy the sneakers. At the store, he bumps into Scott Saver, who pulls out his wallet and pays for the sneakers with the money he saved up. Six months later, when the sneakers are all beat up, Barry is still worrying about how to pay back all his debts, while Scott is busy saving up for his next pair. "Savings are a loan to yourself," Scott says.

   EXPLAIN WHAT SCOTT MEANS. ____________

2. Eventually, Barry Borrower's friends get sick of lending him money. So he goes out and gets himself a credit card. "It's a great thing," he tells his friend Scott. "I don't need to borrow anymore. I never run out of money."
   "That's what you think," Scott says. "A credit card is just a fancy way of borrowing – and you might have to pay lots of interest, too."

   EXPLAIN WHAT SCOTT MEANS. ____________

3. One day, Scott Saver meets Barry Borrower riding a spanking new bike. "Nice bike, Barry," he says. "I know what you're thinking, Scott," Barry says. "And this time, you're wrong! I didn't borrow a penny to buy this bike! I took out an installment plan, and I only have to pay $10 a month for the next 18 months.'
   "Bad deal, Barry," Scott says. "I'm saving up for the same bike, but it's only going to cost me $140. And besides, you may not have borrowed from me, but you did borrow from the store."

   A) EXPLAIN WHAT SCOTT MEANS WHEN HE SAYS THAT BARRY DID A BAD DEAL. ____________

   B) EXPLAIN WHAT SCOTT MEANS WHEN HE SAYS THAT BARRY BORROWED FROM THE STORE. ____________

וְנָא אַל תַּצְרִיכֵנוּ ה' אֱלֹקֵינוּ לֹא לִידֵי מַתְּנַת בָּשָׂר וָדָם וְלֹא לִידֵי הַלְוָאָתָם. (ברכת המזון)
Please, Hashem, do not make us needy of the gifts of people or of their loans. (Birkat HaMazon)

15

Workbook: Patty's Plans

Goal

To learn how personal initiative can help people surmount minor financial challenges.

Pat's Plans

A LESSON IN ENTREPRENEURSHIP

PAT PLANNER AND HIS FRIEND CALVIN COPER ARE DREAMING OF TAKING A TRIP TO ERETZ YISRAEL FOR SUCCOT, BUT NEITHER ONE HAS THE MONEY FOR A TICKET.

PAT DECIDES THAT HE'S GOING TO EARN THE MONEY TO PAY FOR HIS TRIP TO ERETZ YISRAEL. THESE ARE THE STEPS HE FOLLOWS:

Step 1: Finding a need that you can fill

"In order to make money," Pat says, "I'll have to think about what people in my neighborhood need that I can provide. There's no tutoring program for the kids in my area, who stay in the city in the summer. I'm a good student and I'm great with kids. It's all about supply and demand – there's a demand for a tutoring program, and if I can supply it, then I'm in business."

Step 2: Market research

"But how do I know that people will want to send their kids to my tutoring program?" Pat wonders. "I better speak to the parents in the area and find out. I also need to find out what the going prices are fo
teenager in other parts of the neighborhood."

Step 3: Pricing

"Let's see," says Pat. "I'm hoping to earn at least $1,200 this summer to cover my ticket. How's this going to work?

Considerations:

A. Cost of running a 3-week tutoring program – 5 nights a week:

Renting space in a shul 3 hours a night for 3 weeks: $400
Treats/ prizes: $40 a child (fluctuating expense, depending on number of children)
Advertising: $80 (one-time expense)
Assistant tutor: $620 (fixed expense)

B. Breakeven point:

Option 1:
If I charge each student $150, ($10 an hour per student in each group, 1 hour a night, 5 nights a we
have 10 kids in my tutoring program just to cover my expenses and break even. After that, each
will represent $110 in profit.

Pat's Plans cont'd

That means that if I charge $150, my breakeven point is 10 kids, or $1500.
10 x $40 (cost per student) + $400 (rent) + $620 (assistant) +$80 (advertising) = $1500

Option 2:
If I charge each student $225, ($15 an hour per student in each group, 1 hour a night, 5 nights a week) I'll need to have just 6 kids in my tutoring program to cover my expenses and break even. After that, each additional kid will represent $185 in profit.
That means that if I charge $225, my breakeven point is 6 kids, or $1350:
6 x $40 (cost per kid) + $400 (rent) + $620 (assistant) + $80 (advertising) = $1340 (with $10 to spare)

C. Profit:

In order to save up $1200 for my trip, I need to earn $1200 more than my breakeven point. That means that:

If I charge $150 per kid, I'll need 21 kids in my tutoring program: 10 to break even, and another 11 to profit.

Total revenue: 21 x $150 = $3150
Total expenses: 21 x $40 + $400 + $620 + $80 = $1940
Profit: $3150 - $1940 = $1210

If I charge $225 per kid, I'll need 13 kids in my tutoring program: 6 to break even, and another 7 to profit.

Total revenue: 13 x $225 = $2925
Total expenses: 13 x $40 + $400 + $620 + $80 = $1620
Profit: $2925 - $1620 = $1305

D. Pricing:

"The other tutoring programs in the neighborhood are charging between $180 and $300 for the three-week period," says Pat. "It would be nice to charge less than everyone else, but I don't think it's realistic for me to get the 21 kids I need in order to pay for my ticket, and I wouldn't have enough hours in the evening to teach them either. So I think I'll charge $225, and aim to get at least 15 kids: 6 to break even, another 7 to profit, and another 2 to cover maaser and unexpected expenses. If I get fewer kids than that, it's not worth opening."

Step 4: Marketing

"Now it's time to get the word out," says Pat Planner. "We're going to run a three-pronged campaign: posters, phone calls and advertisements." He prints up signs and hangs them all around, and puts an ad into the local advertising circular. Then he starts making phone calls – not just to the parents in the area, but to anyone he knows. "It's called networking," Pat says. "The more people who know about my tutoring program, the more customers I'll have."

Step 5: Do it - and do it right

"Great," says Pat. "I have 16 kids signed up for my tutoring program. That means I'll even have a bit of extra money to treat them to a fun pizza party at the end – and make sure they'll want to come back next summer. Eretz Yisrael, here I come!"

FIVE CHEERS FOR PAT!

LOOK AT ALL THE GREAT THINGS PAT DID!

1. He earned herself the opportunity to visit Eretz Yisrael.
2. He helped 16 kids catch up with their learning and feel good about themselves.
3. He helped 16 sets of parents give their kids a boost for next year.
4. He gave *maaser* on the money he earned.

AND LAST BUT NOT LEAST:

5. He gave his friend Sammy Schnorrer a job as his assistant so that Sammy would have his own money and wouldn't have to ask others for money anymore. Pat, did you know that giving someone a job is the highest form of tzedakah?

Workbook: Assignment/Class Activity: Class Tzedakah Campaign

Goal

To learn how to implement the steps of responsible business planning.

Class Tzedakah Campaign

Challenge

Your class is going to raise money to donate something that your school needs.

A tzedakah campaign such as this should be built in keeping with the same principles as any business venture. In order to run a successful campaign, therefore, you will need to come up with workable business idea and build a plan for getting the idea off the ground.

STEP 1: FINDING A NEED THAT YOU CAN FILL

Brainstorm – supply and demand:
What products or services are in demand in your community that your class can supply in order to earn money to help your school?

STEP 2: MARKET RESEARCH

Ask your family, neighbors, and friends:

- Would they be willing to pay for the product or service your class is thinking of providing?
- Who else in your community is providing that same product or service?
- Is there room for more people to provide that product or service?
- What is the going rate for what you'd like to provide?

STEP 3: PRICING

Cost

- What type of expenses will you have? (Supplies, advertising, manpower, overhead, e
- How much will each type of expense cost you?
- Which expenses will you have no matter how much you sell (fixed costs)?
- Which expenses will go up the more you sell (fluctuating costs)?

Breakeven point

- How much of your product or service will you have to sell in order to cover just the c your venture?

Profit

- How much profit do you need to earn in order to make your venture worthwhile and b the item your school needs?

Pricing

- How much can you charge for your product or service?
- If you charge more, will you lose customers?
- If you charge less, will you gain customers?
- What is the price that will allow you to bring in the most profit?

STEP 4: MARKETING

Get the word out! Some ways to let people know about your product or service:

- Networking: Tell them, and ask them to tell other people.
- Hang up signs and posters
- Make phone calls
- Advertise in local circulars
- Direct mail

STEP 5: DO IT – AND DO IT RIGHT!

When you provide a product or service, you have to be a professional. That means:

- You keep careful accounts of the money, so that you know exactly how much came in and how much went out. (Otherwise, it is impossible to know how much you've earned.)
- You keep the money of your venture separate from your own money.
- What you do, you do well, without cutting corners.
- You take responsibility for your product or service, and make sure that the customer is satisfied.
- If things go wrong (and they often do), you keep a smile on your face and deal with the situation maturely, without looking to blame others.

HERE ARE SOME IDEAS OF PRODUCTS AND SERVICES YOU CAN PROVIDE IN ORDER TO RAISE MONEY FOR YOUR SCHOOL:

- After-school clubs
- Chanukah/Purim carnival
- Cheesecake for Shavuot
- Cookbook
- Erev Pesach car cleaning service
- Mishloach Manot
- Raffle
- Selling popcorn, lemonade, cholent, etc.
- Tu b'Shvat platters

GOOD LUCK!

UNIT 3

KIDS' NEEDS AND WANTS

Unit 3

Kids' Needs and Wants

Educational goals

1. *To identify the causes of the "I want it now" syndrome and recognize its damaging effects.*
2. *To introduce the relationship (or lack thereof) between possessions and happiness.*
3. *To coach students on how to communicate their needs and wants to parents and teachers, respectfully and effectively.*
4. *To discover why people begin to need things that were not necessary before.*

Materials

- 1 lesson plan for teacher
- Workbook Pages:
  - Kids & stores
  - Kids and Stores: Review
  - Let's Try That Again, Okay?
  - The Thneed Syndrome
- 1 audio clip: Never Take Kids to a Store

To the teacher

The Ever-Expanding Balloon of Basic Needs

Unprecedented Prosperity

By historical standards, our generation is blessed with unprecedented prosperity. Even the poor among us enjoy luxuries that were unheard of a century ago (think indoor plumbing, refrigerators, telephones). Today, basic living standards have ballooned to the extent that a child who has one Shabbat outfit, or doesn't go to summer camp or daycamp, is living well beneath the standards of almost any frum community in the world, and might legitimately be considered a deprived kid.

Is this a positive development or a negative one? Well, on the one hand, it's definitely a wonderful blessing that we can provide our children with not just the basics, but also with comforts and conveniences that make their lives – and ours – so much more pleasant.

On the other hand, however, prosperity and comfort carry with them the inherent danger of raising expectations, which lead to feelings of entitlement and make kids (and adults, too) *feel* deprived even when, relatively speaking, they are extremely fortunate. When we speak of children being "spoiled," what we mean is that they are so showered with comforts and luxuries that they can hardly appreciate what they have.

Therefore, as educators and parents, we need to find the correct balance that will allow us to benefit from the prosperity that surrounds us, while not allowing that prosperity to turn us into soft, indulged, needy people whose happiness is entirely dependent on external circumstances and *things*. If we wish to raise a generation of young people with strong characters and idealistic goals, we have to teach them to question the ever-expanding balloon of basic necessities, and give them the tools to maintain control over their needs and wants, instead of being controlled by those needs and wants.

We're on the Same Side

How can we convey this in the classroom?

With a light touch.

Even at this age, children are sick of hearing lectures about how spoiled today's generation is, and how "When I was a kid, I only had…" Nor are they open to hearing tirades about the evils of materialism and the wonders of austerity.

In order to convey these concepts effectively, we have to strip them of any judgmental or emotional tone and aim for an objective, original, and "We're on the same side" presentation.

In the handouts included in this unit, we have attempted to get at the core of why kids think that they need things, and also to help them improve the way they communicate their desires. The educational challenge in this unit is to get the kids to examine their own thought processes *without condemning them in any way*, and allow them to reach conclusions about their own behavior *independently*.

Workbook: Kids' Needs and Wants

Goal

To humorously portray some of the negative ways in which children express their desires, and help students to understand the roots of these behaviors.

Unit 3 | Kids' Needs and Wants

Kids and Stores

Introduction

All people need and want things. Kids often don't have the ability to buy their own stuff, which means that they turn to their parents for what they need or want.
Parents want to give to their children, but sometimes they can't, and sometimes they choose not to, for various reasons (for example, they'll tell you that too much candy is bad for your teeth). As adults with life experience, they understand that love means saying no sometimes.
When you need or want something, what do you do? Let's look at what you don't do:

Song:

NEVER TAKE KIDS TO A STORE

Marvelous Midos Machine Volume III, by Abie Rotenberg (used with permission)

I met my good friend Mr. Katz yesterday
He looked all upset, so I started to say
Things can't be so bad, why are you so sad
You better tell me right away

I'd be just as happy as I was before
If only I'd listened and trusted you more
I ignored your advice, now I'm paying the price
I went with all of my kids TO A STORE!

You went to a store with your girls and your boys?
And it was a big store, a store filled with toys
But I warned you not, I know I forgot
Oy it was a day that I did not enjoy

I know just what happened don't tell me a thing
I know 'cause I took my kids there last spring
When you got to the store and walked through the door
All of your kinderlach started to SING:

We want Lego and Construx
And a hockey set deluxe
We want baseballs we want bats
We want helmets we want hats
Like I said to you before, never take kids to a store
All you're gonna hear is, we want more and more

Tatty there's a pretty doll with shiny golden hair
I'm sorry little shayfela am I a millionaire?
You already have that train, I know it works just fine
But look it's such a bargain only $19.99

We want cars and trucks you see
And of course Monopoly
See this camera it's so nice
Look it's made by Fisher Price
Like I said to you before, never take kids to a store
All you're gonna hear is, we want more and more

Why do you need that Care Bear?
There's one at home I think
But Tatty that one's yellow and this one is pink
Do you see this storybook it's something that I need
I'd love to buy it Shmuly,
BUT YOU DON'T KNOW HOW TO READ!

We want robots that can talk
And animals that walk
We want checkers we want chess
WE WON'T EVER LEAVE A MESS!
Like I said to you before, never take kids to a store
All you're gonna hear is, we want more and more

They were crying, they were shouting,
why I'll bet one even screamed
And you whispered, please be quiet,
we don't want to make a scene
So you bought them all they wanted,
more than you can afford
And an hour after you got home, they said....
TATTY WE ARE BORED!

But kids who have good middos,
are simply not that way
They know how to appreciate whatever comes their way
And you can even disregard all that I've said before
And let them come along with you
When - you - go - to - a - store.

23

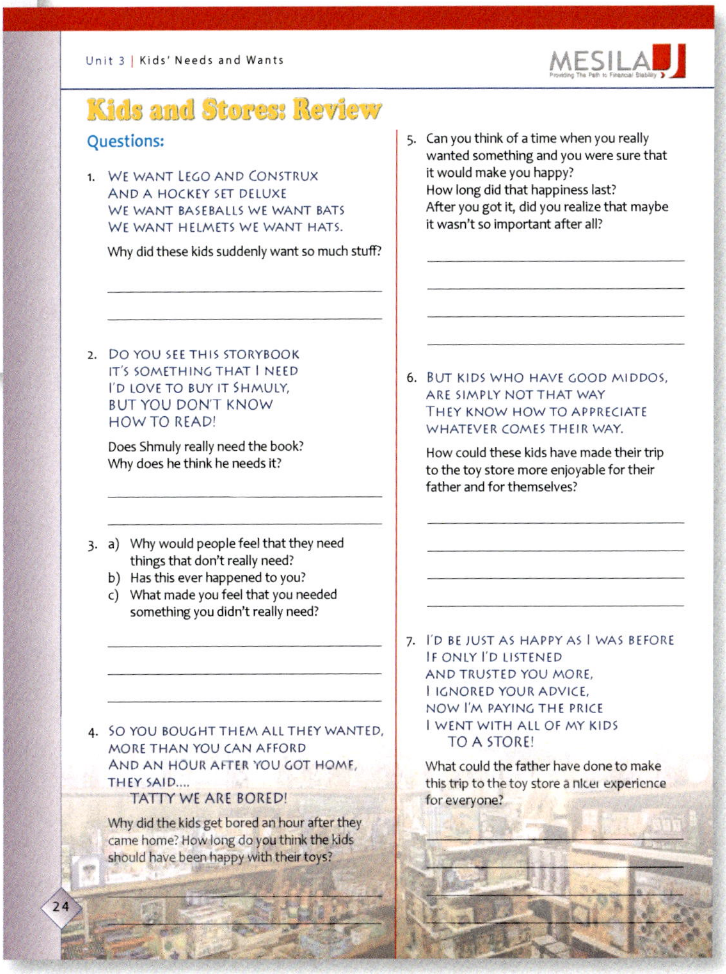

Unit 3 | Kids' Needs and Wants

Kids and Stores: Review

Questions:

1. WE WANT LEGO AND CONSTRUX
AND A HOCKEY SET DELUXE
WE WANT BASEBALLS WE WANT BATS
WE WANT HELMETS WE WANT HATS.
Why did these kids suddenly want so much stuff?

2. DO YOU SEE THIS STORYBOOK
IT'S SOMETHING THAT I NEED
I'D LOVE TO BUY IT SHMULY,
BUT YOU DON'T KNOW
HOW TO READ!
Does Shmuly really need the book?
Why does he think he needs it?

3. a) Why would people feel that they need things that don't really need?
b) Has this ever happened to you?
c) What made you feel that you needed something you didn't really need?

4. SO YOU BOUGHT THEM ALL THEY WANTED,
MORE THAN YOU CAN AFFORD
AND AN HOUR AFTER YOU GOT HOME,
THEY SAID....
TATTY WE ARE BORED!
Why did the kids get bored an hour after they came home? How long do you think the kids should have been happy with their toys?

5. Can you think of a time when you really wanted something and you were sure that it would make you happy?
How long did that happiness last?
After you got it, did you realize that maybe it wasn't so important after all?

6. BUT KIDS WHO HAVE GOOD MIDDOS,
ARE SIMPLY NOT THAT WAY
THEY KNOW HOW TO APPRECIATE
WHATEVER COMES THEIR WAY.
How could these kids have made their trip to the toy store more enjoyable for their father and for themselves?

7. I'D BE JUST AS HAPPY AS I WAS BEFORE
IF ONLY I'D LISTENED
AND TRUSTED YOU MORE,
I IGNORED YOUR ADVICE,
NOW I'M PAYING THE PRICE
I WENT WITH ALL OF MY KIDS
TO A STORE!
What could the father have done to make this trip to the toy store a nicer experience for everyone?

24

Workbook:
Let's Try That Again, Okay?

Goal

To help students learn to communicate their needs and wants to parents and teachers, respectfully and effectively.

Let's Try That Again, Okay?

Expressing Your Needs Respectfully & Effectively

OUR FAMILY NEVER DOES ANYTHING FUN.

YOU NEVER BUY ME ANYTHING!

MOMMY, WHY CAN'T YOU BUY ME ONE? EVERYONE ELSE HAS ONE!

YOU PROMISED!

YOU LIKE MY BROTHER BETTER! HE HAS ONE, SO WHY CAN'T I?

Let's try this again.

What would be a nicer way to ask for what you need or want?

1. Make requests, not demands. Your tone of voice, the words you use, and your body language will make the difference between a polite conversation and an argument.
2. Offer to participate in some way, through your own money or effort. ("What if I help you in the garden?" "What if I use the birthday money from Grandma?")
3. Express your needs respectfully, without criticizing or accusing. Explain why it's important for you to have this. "It's important for me to have a knapsack with wheels because I have to go up a big hill." "I feel uncomfortable when I keep borrowing my friend's calculator in math class."
4. Stay away from YOU statements:
"You said/You didn't/You always/You never/How come you/Only you…"
5. Find a time to ask that's not busy or stressful – DON'T ASK for things an hour before Shabbat, or when your mother or father is on the phone, etc.
6. Before you ask for something, think about whether you really need it. Don't ask for too many things at once.

In the following examples, how could kids communicate their needs more effectively?

☹ "BUT I NEED A NEW PAIR OF GOGGLES! EVERYONE ELSE HAS SPEEDO!"

☺ ______________________________

☹ "IT'S NOT FAIR! EVERY TIME WE GO ON A SCHOOL TRIP I HAVE TO COPY PICTURES FROM MY FRIENDS' CAMERAS BECAUSE MY CAMERA TAKES SUCH LOUSY PICTURES. WHY CAN'T YOU BUY ME A BETTER CAMERA?"

☺ ______________________________

☹ "YOU PROMISED US EXTRA RECESS! ALL THE OTHER TEACHERS LET THEIR CLASS STAY OUT AFTER THE BELL."

☺ ______________________________

Workbook:
The Thneed Syndrome

Goal

To understand how new needs are created.

The Thneed Syndrome

CREATING NEEDS & WANTS WHERE NONE EXISTED

How do people start needing things that they didn't need before?

1. **Technological advances**
EXAMPLE: 100 years ago people didn't need telephones or washing machines.
2. **Rise in standard of living / social pressure**
EXAMPLE: 100 years ago people had only one Shabbat outfit and one weekday outfit.
3. **Advertising**
EXAMPLE: The De Beers diamond company coined the slogan "A diamond is forever" in 1947, turning diamonds into a symbol of engagement. Today, every kallah needs a diamond ring. It wasn't always this way!
4. **Affluence**
EXAMPLE: When people have extra money to spend, they look for new things to spend it on, such as fancier vacations and more gourmet food, and eventually these things become needs.

Here's an illustration of how a need is created:

In a book called ***The Lorax***, by Dr. Seuss, a fellow opens a factory for a new type of garment called a "Thneed," and a creature named the Lorax ridicules him for creating this useless item.

To which the fellow responds:

*"A Thneed's a fine something that all people need!
It's a shirt. It's a sock. It's a glove. It's a hat.
But it has other uses. Yes, far beyond that.
You can use it for carpets. For pillows! For sheets!
Or curtains! Or covers for bicycle seats!"*

*The Lorax said, "Sir! You are crazy with greed.
There is no one on earth
who would buy that fool Thneed!"
But the very next minute I proved he was wrong.
For, just at that minute, a chap came along,
and he thought that the Thneed I had knitted was great.
He happily bought it for three ninety-eight.*

*I laughed at the Lorax, "You poor [silly] guy!
You never can tell what some people will buy."*

Can you think of any "Thneeds" that you have?
(i.e., items that have no real use or value but are considered important or essential)

UNIT 4

BUDGETING

Unit 4

Budgeting

Educational goals

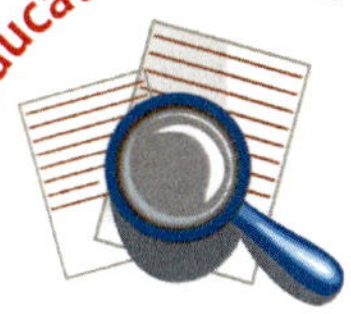

1. *To realize that time, energy, and money are G-d-given tools.*
2. *To learn how to allocate time and money in the way that is most beneficial.*
3. *To internalize the principle that you can't spend more than you have.*
4. *To identify what's more important and less important to acquire.*
5. *To understand that a budget is as much about what you can have as about what you can't have.*
6. *To learn how to build a real-life budget.*

Materials

- 2 lesson plans for teacher
- Workbook pages:
  - **Amusement park exercise**
  - **School supplies price list**
  - **Budgeting exercise - Pack Your Knapsack**
- PowerPoint presentation: **Budget Your Budget** (Review)

Lesson 1

Lesson 1: Introduction to Budgeting

The Time ➤ Energy ➤ Money Triangle

A. Hashem gives us what we need so that we can accomplish everything we are supposed to accomplish in our life. He gives us all the tools that are necessary, and it's up to us to use these tools in the best way possible. That means that we have to plan how to use the tools we have carefully.

B. There are three main kinds of tools that Hashem gives us:

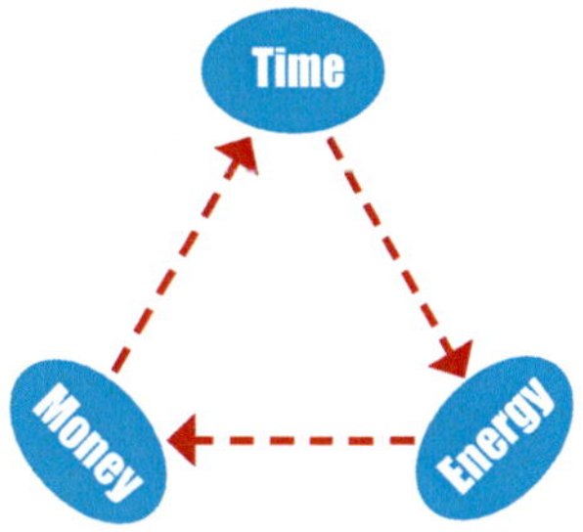

C. These three types of tools are necessary to accomplish anything we want to do. *Examples:*

a. Preparing for Shabbat

b. Going on vacation

c. Making a wedding

D. To do any of these things, you need to invest **time**, **energy**, and **money**. Since you have a limited amount of time, energy, and money, you have to plan how to use these resources in the most efficient way possible.

Explanatory notes to teacher:

1. Budgeting is a skill that is useful for managing any type of resource. In trying to teach children how to budget their money, we first want to impart to them the general skill of budgeting their time, because time is something that they are already familiar with. The principles are transferable, and after learning how to budget time, they can use this skill to budget money.

2. The following exercise is designed to develop and strengthen budgeting skills without involving money at all, because money is a very emotionally laden concept. When people think of budgeting money, they think of what they "can't afford," which automatically makes them tense. That's why many people – many adults – avoid budgeting. But the truth is that practically every decision a person makes involves budgeting skills: if I choose this, I have to give up that. Once this concept is introduced, we can then apply it to money.

3. The children should be taught that the reason they can't have everything isn't because "there's not enough money" – it's because nobody can have everything and you have to make choices. The purpose of a budget is not to deprive you – it's to help you get the things you want *most*. This concept is very effectively demonstrated using time as a commodity, rather than money – everyone understands intuitively that you have a limited amount of time, and this limitation is not *bad*, it is simply a structure into which you have to fit everything you want to do. Similarly, in budgeting your money, you have to fit all the items you want into the structure of the money you have.

Pizza Time

A. A pizza pie can be divided any number of ways, but you can't get more pizza in the pie than there is. **That's what budgeting is all about: slicing up the pie.**

B. Your time is your pizza. It's your pie – you decide how to slice it!

Workbook: Amusement Park Activity

Goal

To learn to budget effectively using time as the unit of currency.

Instructions to teacher

The page entitled **"Amusement Park Activity"** should be photocopied and handed out to the students. The students should be divided into pairs, with each pair responsible for completing the activity. (Alternatively, the activity can be done as an interactive class exercise, guided by the teacher.)

Questions for discussion

a) How much time did you spend waiting?
b) How much time did you spend on rides?
c) Which rides did you feel were worth the wait?
d) Which rides were not worth the wait?
e) Did you go on the rides/attractions that didn't have any wait? Why or why not?

Optional class discussion

The things that are worth more to people usually come at a higher cost. Some rides have more wait time to ride time, while some have less.

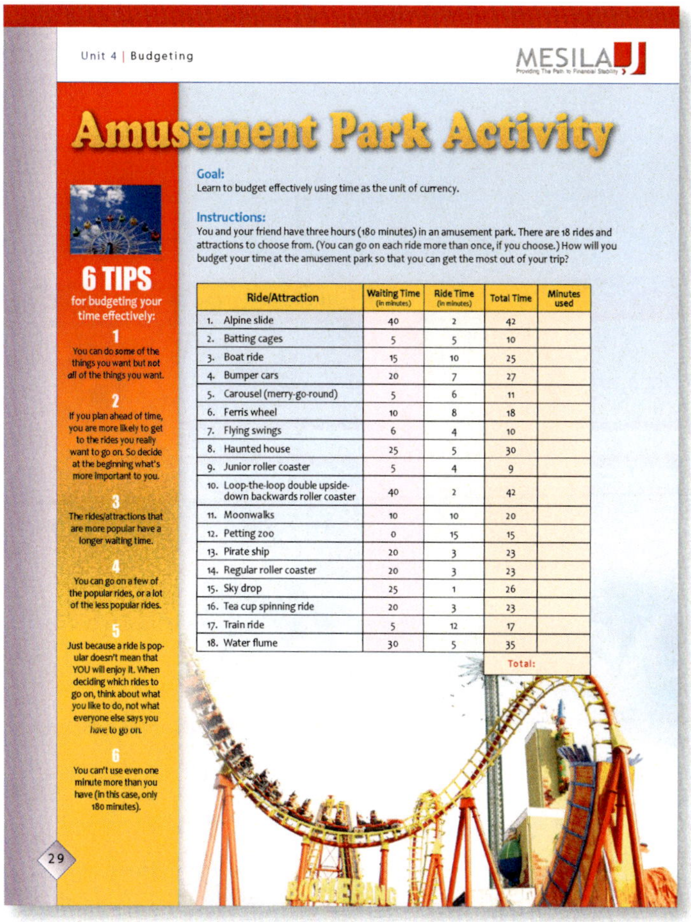

Unit 4 | Budgeting

Amusement Park Activity

6 TIPS for budgeting your time effectively:

1. You can do *some* of the things you want but *not all* of the things you want.
2. If you plan ahead of time, you are more likely to get to the rides you really want to go on. So decide at the beginning what's more important to you.
3. The rides/attractions that are more popular have a longer waiting time.
4. You can go on a few of the popular rides, or a lot of the less popular rides.
5. Just because a ride is popular doesn't mean that YOU will enjoy it. When deciding which rides to go on, think about what *you* like to do, not what everyone else says you *have* to go on.
6. You can't use even one minute more than you have (in this case, only 180 minutes).

Goal:
Learn to budget effectively using time as the unit of currency.

Instructions:
You and your friend have three hours (180 minutes) in an amusement park. There are 18 rides and attractions to choose from. (You can go on each ride more than once, if you choose.) How will you budget your time at the amusement park so that you can get the most out of your trip?

Ride/Attraction	Waiting Time (in minutes)	Ride Time (in minutes)	Total Time	Minutes used
1. Alpine slide	40	2	42	
2. Batting cages	5	5	10	
3. Boat ride	15	10	25	
4. Bumper cars	20	7	27	
5. Carousel (merry-go-round)	5	6	11	
6. Ferris wheel	10	8	18	
7. Flying swings	6	4	10	
8. Haunted house	25	5	30	
9. Junior roller coaster	5	4	9	
10. Loop-the-loop double upside-down backwards roller coaster	40	2	42	
11. Moonwalks	10	10	20	
12. Petting zoo	0	15	15	
13. Pirate ship	20	3	23	
14. Regular roller coaster	20	3	23	
15. Sky drop	25	1	26	
16. Tea cup spinning ride	20	3	23	
17. Train ride	5	12	17	
18. Water flume	30	5	35	
			Total:	

29

For instance, you can wait 10 minutes to jump on the moonwalk for 10 minutes or you can wait 40 minutes to ride on the loop-the-loop double upside-down backwards roller coaster for 2 minutes. What's more worthwhile?

That depends on you!

Pizza Time - Again!

Now that the students have absorbed the concept of budgeting time, we are going to apply the same skill to budgeting money:

- Time is a limited resource. Because there's a lot to do in a limited amount of time, you want to use your time as wisely as possible to accomplish the maximum in the time you have. If you plan how to budget your time, you are more likely to use it in way that is most beneficial. "If you fail to plan, you plan to fail."
- Money is also a limited resource. You have lots of things to spend it on, but only a certain amount to spend. If you use it wisely, you can get the most out if it.
- Your money is also your pizza.
  It's your pie – you decide how to slice it!
- A pizza pie can be divided any number of ways, but you can't get more pizza in the pie than there is. That's what budgeting is all about: slicing up the pie.
- Real-life application: You have $50 from your grandparents. What are you going to do with it?
- Draw three (or more) large circles on the board representing the $50 and slice them differently, such as in the following examples:

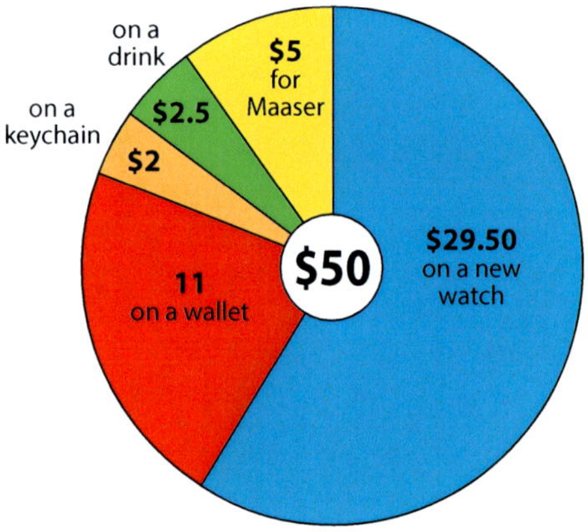

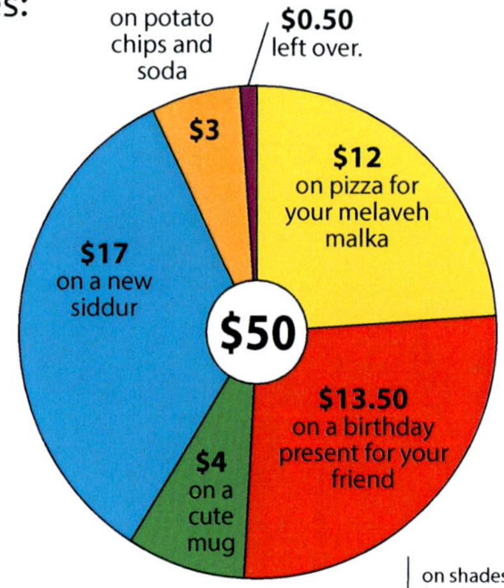

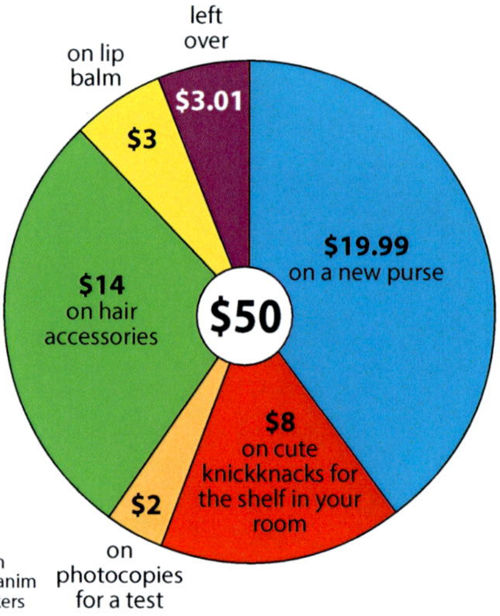

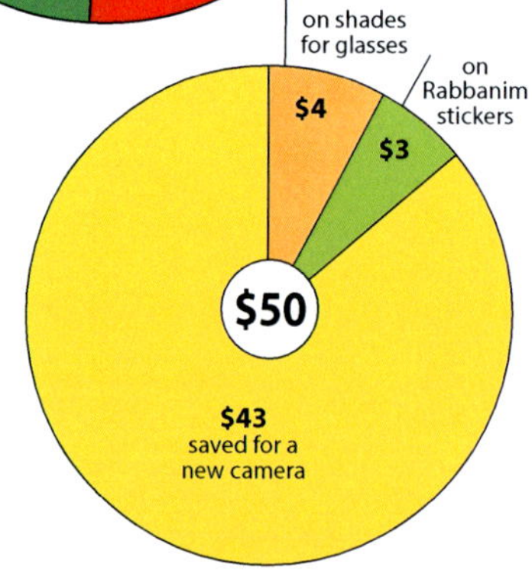

In our next lesson, we will learn how to build a real budget, ***using money*** *instead of* ***time*** *as the currency.*

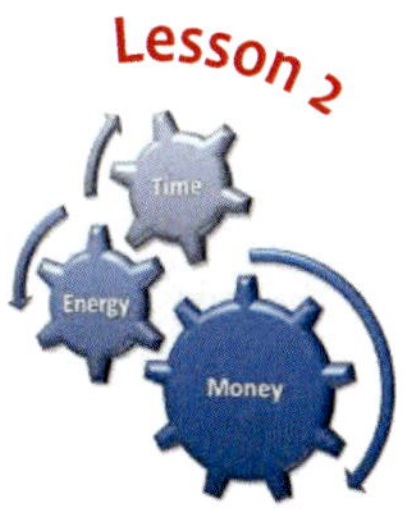

Lesson 2: Hands-On Budgeting

What's a *budget*?

A. The word budget is used in two different ways.

1. **Definition #1:** ***A plan for using the money that you have to get what you need or want.***
2. *Examples:*
   a. "The G.O. prepared a budget for its Chol Hamoed activities."
   b. "The workers submitted an operating budget to the president of the company for the upcoming year."
3. **Definition #2:** ***The amount of money available to be used for a specific purpose.***
4. *Examples:*
   a. "I was able to buy two new outfits with the budget my mother gave me to go shopping."
   b. "I put away my babysitting money for a few months so that I would have a budget to use for canteen in the summer."

B. The two steps of budgeting

1. Part of budgeting is determining how much money is available to you to create your budget plan (definition #2).
2. Part of budgeting is creating a budget plan in order to use your money in the most efficient way possible (definition #1).

C. Is a budget restrictive, or empowering?

People often consider a budget to be restrictive, but the truth is that having a budget actually helps you get what you need and want. If you have a budget for something, it means you can spend money on it. Without a budget, you either have no money to spend, or you don't know how much you have to spend.

It's important to impart to the students a positive association with the concept of budgeting, by focusing on how a budget is empowering.

Workbook: Pack Your Knapsack Budgeting Activity (In-class)

In this exercise, you will be preparing a budget plan (definition #1) using the budget that you are given (definition #2).

Goals

1. To learn to budget effectively using money as the unit of currency.
2. To discover how to use your money in a way that is most beneficial to you.

Instructions to Teacher

The students are given a budget of $55 with which to purchase school supplies for a new school year. They are given a list of school supplies to purchase, along with a price list. The price list includes three prices for each item: a "basic price," a "medium price," and a "high price." The $55 that we have allocated for the students' budget is slightly more than the total cost of all the items in the "medium price" category. This will allow students to choose some items in the high-priced category, but will compel them to keep many of their choices in the basic and medium price range. This teaches them to plan how to use their money in a way that works best for them. (You may choose to assign a different amount of money, but bear in mind that the activity will not work well if kids do not have enough leverage to purchase items in any of the three categories. For the sake of the activity, they have to be able to take all the options into account.)

Divide class into pairs or groups. Each group has to come up with a budget based on the prices in the school supplies list. The budget has to reflect the group's collective choices of what constitutes getting the most value for your money. After the groups build their budgets, each one will present to the class their list of choices, and explain why they think this was the best way to spend their money.

Questions for class discussion & review of activity

1. For which items did you decide to purchase the cheapest option?
2. Why did you feel that it was not worthwhile to spend more on those items?
3. For which items did you decide to purchase the most expensive option?
4. Why did you feel that it was worthwhile to spend more on those items?
5. Which items did you have to compromise on in order to stay within your budget?
6. Do you feel that this budget was fair? Too restrictive? Too generous?
7. Was it difficult to spend all your money? Would you have been able to stay within a smaller budget?

MESILA
Providing The Path to Financial Stability

Unit 4 | Budgeting

MESILA

6 TIPS for budgeting your money effectively:

1
You can have some of the things you want but not all of the things you want. That means you will have to choose some cheaper items and some more expensive items.

2
If you plan well, you are more likely to get the types of supplies you really want. So decide at the beginning what's more important to you.

3
The items that people want more usually come at a higher cost.

4
You can get a few more expensive items, or a lot of cheaper items.

5
Just because a name brand is popular doesn't mean that YOU will like it. When deciding which items to buy, think about what you like to have, not what everyone else says you *have* to have.

6
You can't use even one penny more than you have.

Pack Your Knapsack: Budgeting Activity

Goal:
To learn to budget your money effectively.

Instructions:
You are given $55 to spend on school supplies for the new year. Using the price list provided on the next page, choose which supplies you would like to purchase. Decide which items you want to buy in the "basic price" category, which you want to buy in the "medium price" category, and which you want to buy in the "high price" category.

Rules for this Activity:
1. You need to buy every item on the list.
2. You cannot spend a penny more than you have.
3. You are allowed to keep up to $2 of the money if you go under budget. The rest of the money needs to be used.

Item	Description	Cost
Crayons		
Eraser		
Folder		
Glue		
Looseleaf		
Markers		
Spiral notebook		
Pens		
Pencil case		
Lead pencils		
Ruler		
Scissors		
	TOTAL:	

30

eting

MESILA

ck Your apsack: geting Activity

Price List

Item	Basic Price (Rock-Bottom)	Manufacturer Name / Description	Medium Price (Middle-of-the-Road)	Manufacturer Name / Description	High Price (The Best)	Manufacturer Name / Description
Crayons	$1	No brand, 10 crayons	$3	Crayola 24 crayons	$8	Crayola 98 crayons with sharpener
Eraser	$0.50	Plain white	$1.50	Cartoon figure, bubble-gum smell	$3	Extra big with brush and case
Folder	$1	Standard, one-color	$3.50	Mead five-star	$7	Paul Frank with Julius the monkey
Glue	$1	Shoprite brand	$2	Elmer's school glue	$5	Sparkly Elmer's
Looseleaf	$3	Plain, no name	$8	Staples easy-open looseleaf with plastic front for inserting pictures	$20	Avery D-ring heavy-duty easy-to-open
Markers	$2	8 RoseArt markers	$6	10 Crayola markers	$13	24 highligher Sharpies
Spiral notebook	$1	Plain spiral, Walmart Great Value	$4	Mead five-star	$16	Juicy Couture
Pens	$2	Package of 6 plain ballpoint Bic pens	$4	Pilot G2 pens (6)	$8	10 gel pens
Pencil case	$4	Plain, one-color, one zipper	$8	All-zipper cute one	$15	Kipling with hanging monkey
Lead pencil	$1	Regular no-name lead pencil	$4	Bic #2 lead pencil	$8	Mechanical personalized lead pencil
Ruler	$0.50	Plastic short	$3	Sturdy, long metal	$7	Long, wooden ruler with built-in hole puncher
Scissors	$1	Small, not so sharp, good enough for paper	$3	Target standard school scissor	$9	Super sharp, easy-to-hold, fancy high-tech colors, blade-guard
Total	**$18.00**		**$50.00**		**$119.00**	

31

8. ***Discussion:***

   Shimon decides that he's going to buy only the basic-price items, and he spends only $18 on all of his school supplies. Do you think this is a good idea? Why or why not?

   (On the one hand, Shimon is saving a lot of money. He has all the supplies he needs, plus money left over to buy a knapsack on sale. On the other hand, he might not be satisfied with the supplies he has. They might break and need to be replaced. They might not work well.)

9. ***Situation:***

   While you're in the store you remember that you need construction paper and puff paint for a project you are working on. What changes can you make to your budget to accommodate these items?

PowerPoint presentation:

Budget Your Budget! (unit review)

UNIT 5

SOCIAL RESPONSI-BILITY

Unit 5

Social Responsibility

1. *To empower students to influence others positively rather than be passively dragged along by societal norms.*
2. *To identify external motivations that cause people to want more and spend more.*
3. *To value discretion and develop a respect for boundaries and privacy in the financial realm, both one's own and others.*
4. *To encourage students to avoid conspicuous consumption and not to call attention to themselves through their possessions.*

A. Social Responsibility: Introduction

As important as it is to teach children about not succumbing to negative peer pressure, the purpose of this class is really to introduce the idea that children can exert positive peer pressure on others, not just be passive "victims" of the peer pressure they experience. Rather than be influenced, or feel pressured by the standards set by others, they can be empowered to have confidence in themselves unrelated to their belongings and develop a sense of social responsibility that will prevent them from unwittingly creating unhealthy pressure among their peers.

Materials:

- 1 lesson plan
- Workbook pages:
  Social Responsibility: Scenarios 1-14
- Activity: Social Responsibility: Your Scenario

B. Real-Life Scenarios

Workbook: Social Responsibility Scenarios

Each of the following scenarios is designed to challenge your students and spark discussion. Each scenario is followed by questions for discussion. In the teacher's guide, answers and commentary appear to the right of the scenarios to help you guide the discussion in the desired direction. You may choose to use all of the scenarios or select those that are appropriate for your class.

The scenarios appear in the accompanying handout, without the answers. You can use these scenarios in the following ways:

1) **Class discussion:** Teacher presents each scenario, and then poses questions to the class, going through the scenarios one by one.

2) **Group work:** Divide the class into groups. Each group receives a copy of the scenarios and discusses each one, then answers the relevant questions. Teacher subsequently reviews and summarizes each scenario with the entire class.

3) **Skits:** Divide the class into pairs or groups (depending on the number of students in the class) and have each group prepare a scenario, act it out, and then pose the questions that follow to the class, with the teacher moderating. The students may prepare the scenarios in advance and bring props to dramatize their presentation.

1a. A Real Bar Mitzvah - Part 1 Joey's parents want to make him a simple bar mitzvah. Some of Joey's friends have simple bar mitzvahs, and others have more lavish affairs. Joey wants a more lavish bar mitzvah. His parents offer that he can use the money that will come in as bar mitzvah gifts to upgrade to a fancier bar mitzvah. Joey is in a dilemma. Then, he goes to his friend Sauli's bar mitzvah, which is a really simple event. At that bar mitzvah, his other friend Meir looks around and says, "It just doesn't feel like a real bar mitzvah." What do you think Joey decided? Was there anything wrong with what Meir said? Don't we all speak that way sometimes? Do we realize the implications of our casual observations?	SCENARIO 1A ANSWERS AND THOUGHTS *If Joey was unsure, Meir's comment would likely have pushed him in the direction of paying for the fancier bar mitzvah with his own bar mitzvah money. After all, who doesn't want a "real" bar mitzvah?*
1b. A Real Bar Mitzvah - Part 2 Simon, who is sitting on the other side of Meir, whispers to Meir, "I think Joey might be having his bar mitzvah here too. You might have made him feel bad." "What difference does it make to Joey?" Meir scoffs. "If this is where he's planning to have his bar mitzvah, he shouldn't care about what I say." Meir doesn't realize the power he has. How would he feel if he knew that Joey used his own bar mitzvah money just to avoid Meir's disapproval?	SCENARIO 1B ANSWERS AND THOUGHTS *We can all think of casual comments that hurt us in a way that the people who made the comments would never have dreamed. Let's be more careful with what we say and be aware of our own power to affect people with words or even gestures.*

2. A Pretzel By Any Other Name Tastes the Same A big bag of pretzels costs $1.99 and contains enough snack for 10 recesses (20 cents each). Individual snack-size bags of the same pretzels costs $4.99 for a package of 10 (50 cents each). Moshe's mother bought the big bags of pretzels and gave them out to Moshe and his four brothers and sisters: 5 kids x 180 school days x 20 cents = $180 over the course of the school year (if you buy only the big bags) 5 kids x 180 school days x 50 cents = $450 over the course of the school year (if you buy only the individual packets) That's a difference of $270 – just for morning recess! If you were buying snacks, which ones would you buy? Could you see any reason why someone else might buy the other type? Why isn't Moshe happy with the snacks he gets? What could Moshe's friends do to make him feel happier? What could Moshe tell himself to make himself happier?	SCENARIO 2 ANSWERS AND THOUGHTS *The reason Moshe is unhappy with his snacks is because he is comparing his snacks to what the other kids have, not because there's something wrong with his snack (even if he does convince himself that pretzels in a snack bag are crunchier). If Moshe's friends wouldn't think there's something wrong with his snacks, then that attitude would trickle over to Moshe as well – even if it is unspoken. If Moshe would realize that it's okay not to have what other people have, he might feel better about his snacks, too. He might even bring an extra-large bag of homemade popcorn to give out to his friends.*
3. In Fairness to Others Mrs. Cohen goes shopping for a new backpack with her third-grader, Mark. Mark immediately chooses the most expensive, designer-label backpack in the store. There are another two backpacks that he also likes, but not as much. The fancy backpack is usually double the price of the others, but now it is on sale for only $15 more than the regular ones. Mrs. Cohen can afford it, but she tells Mark that she is not buying it. "But Ma," Mark begs. "My friend Rubi just got that backpack! Why doesn't Mrs. Cohen want to buy the more expensive backpack?	SCENARIO 3 ANSWERS AND THOUGHTS *Mrs. Cohen knows that if Rubi has the backpack, AND Mark gets it, the other kids in the class will feel tremendous pressure to have the backpack too – and they will beg their parents even more. Some parents can't afford it, and even those who can, wouldn't need it if not for the fact that a few kids in the class have it.*
4. Check Out My Camera Eli is going to Camp Achvah this summer and wants to make a good impression on his bunkmates. When he unpacks, he leaves his suitcase open on his bed just long enough for everyone in the bunk to see his brand new, top-of-the-line digital camera. Why might this be unfair to the other boys in the bunk? Why might this be unfair to Eli?	SCENARIO 4 ANSWERS AND THOUGHTS *Maybe the other kids don't have or can't afford it.* *Maybe the other kids will become his friends because they like his camera and not because they actually like him.*

MESILA Providing The Path to Financial Stability

5a. Less is More - Part 1

Simon saves up the money he earns running errands for the neighbor to buy nice bar-mitzvah presents for his friends. He really wants them to be happy, and he doesn't want to disappoint anyone. But he's finding himself working an awful lot just to keep up with all the bar-mitzvahs. Then, when his bar-mitzvah comes along, his friends chip in together to buy him a single, nice set of sefarim, at a much lower cost per boy. How do you think Simon feels?

SCENARIO 5A ANSWERS AND THOUGHTS

Simon may feel disappointed that the gift was so much cheaper and simpler than the ones he worked so hard to buy his friends for their bar-mitzvahs.

He may also feel insulted that his friends don't care enough about him to buy him something that's worth more.

5b. Less is More - Part 2

Simon is thrilled with the gift, even though it only cost a few dollars. "I'm so relieved," he tells his mother. "I see that I don't have to buy such fancy presents to make my friends happy. Now I don't have to work so many hours."

In what way did Simon's friends give him a much bigger gift than just a bar-mitzvah present?

SCENARIO 5B ANSWERS AND THOUGHTS

Simon's friends give him the comfort of being able to buy them gifts in return that he can easily afford, and took the emphasis off the price of the gift and put in more on the gesture of the gift and the friendship it represents.

6. Backwards Compliment

"Oh, I really like your tie!" David tells Jack. "I saw it on sale for $4.99 last week. I guess that's why the whole world has it!"

David meant to give Jack a compliment. How do you think Jack felt? Do you think he ever wore the tie again? What do you think he said to his mother when he came home?

SCENARIO 6 ANSWERS AND THOUGHTS

Jack probably did not feel very complimented. If he ever wore the tie again, he probably didn't feel very well-dressed in it. He may have even told his mother that he NEVER wants to wear it again, or that he doesn't want to get ANYTHING that's on sale. David could have just said "I like your tie." The End.

7. The Shoes Have to Go

Victor's Shabbat shoes are three months old, still in fine condition but certainly not snazzy and new. Victor is going to sleep over at his friend Yoni's house for Shabbat and wants to look his absolute best. He looks at his Shabbat shoes and suddenly feels that they are completely unwearable and embarrassing. Last Shabbat, he thought they were just fine.

If you were Yoni, and you knew how he felt, what would you say to Victor?

SCENARIO 7 ANSWERS AND THOUGHTS

Very often, the way we look at what we have and the way we decide whether we like what we have is heavily influenced by the way we think others are looking at us. Until now, Victor liked his Shabbat shoes, because he was looking at them through his own eyes. Now that he's looking at them through Yoni's eyes, he really doesn't like them anymore.

If Yoni would tell Victor, "Where'd you get your shoes? I wish I could have those, too," Victor might suddenly discover that he does like his shoes, after all.

8. Mister Popularity Charlie just switched classes and he wants to make friends quickly. On his first day in the new class, he makes sure everyone sees his huge Rebbe sticker collection and costly school supplies. To his surprise, at recess time, he notices that all the boys are crowding around Benny, whose clothes, knapsack, and coat are clearly hand-me-downs. Benny doesn't have any fancy albums to flaunt and he could use a new pair of shoes, Charlie thinks. "Why do they want to be friends with him?" Charlie wonders.	SCENARIO 8 ANSWERS AND THOUGHTS *Benny can't rely on his clothing and stuff to make his classmates like him, so he's left relying on personality – his kind nature, his friendly manner, and his cheerful disposition. His classmates are attracted to HIM, not to what he has.*
9. How to Ruin Someone's Day Fast Isaac's father buys him a chinuch set of arba minim, which Isaac is very proud of – until his friend Shaul sidles over to him and asks, with a glint in his eye, "How much did that set cost?" Under what circumstances would it be okay to ask someone how much something cost?	SCENARIO 9 ANSWERS AND THOUGHTS *Usually, asking how much something costs is a breach of privacy and is bound to make people uncomfortable. If there is a specific purpose in asking, then there might be justification, provided that (1) you have a close relationship with the person and (2) you know the person will not be embarrassed to answer.*
10a. Nothing to Eat - Part 1 In advance of the class trip, Rabbi Feldman, the teacher, announces that the boys should not bring any nosh or spending money on the trip. The school would give out snacks to everyone. During recess, the class was in an uproar. "That's so unfair," Gabriel protests to his friends. "What's wrong with bringing my own pocket money to buy what I want?" Do you think all the kids in the class agree with Gabriel? How might the atmosphere on the bus be different if all the boys would enjoy the same nosh during the trip?	SCENARIO 10 ANSWERS AND THOUGHTS *Lots of boys were secretly relieved that they won't have the pressure to bring nosh or spending money on the trip. They couldn't speak up, of course, but they are grateful to Rabbi Feldman for his sensitivity. On the bus the boys were able to relax and enjoy each other's company, without worrying whether their nosh was up to par or if the amount of spending money they brought would be enough.*

10b. Nothing to Eat - Part 2 Gabriel and a few other boys complain to Rabbi Feldman about the no-nosh, no-money rule. "What if we don't like anything the school gives?" they ask. "We'll starve!" Rabbi Feldman grudgingly agrees that it's okay to bring a little nosh or a few dollars just in case. That evening, the supermarkets are packed with Rabbi Feldman's students, buying "a little" nosh and racking up a big bill. Describe some of the conversations that might have gone on after school that day in their homes.	SCENARIO 10B ANSWERS AND THOUGHTS *"Ma, I can't go on the trip without any nosh. I'll starve!"!* *"Ma, Rabbi Feldman says we HAVE to have at least two nosh for the trip, and $5 just in case."* *"Ma, everyone's for sure going to bring $10."* *"Ma, I can't go on the trip."*
11. Will the Best Bike Please Stand Up? Jason and Abe are participating in a bikeathon to raise money for tzedakah. They know some kids have really cool bikes, and others have plainer bikes. Jason and Abe happen to have better bikes, but they decide to use their older brothers' secondhand bikes so that the kids who don't have nice bikes should feel better. When the conversation turns to how much the boys' bikes cost – "$100! $200! $300!" Jason pipes up, "My bike was $10 at the flea market!" Is anyone going to think less of Jason and Abe for showing up at the bikeathon with second-rate bikes?	SCENARIO 11 ANSWERS AND THOUGHTS *If Jason and Abe are comfortable with their decision and confident with themselves regardless of the bikes they are driving, chances are they will only rise in their friends' estimation. Who knows? Maybe old bikes will become the new rage.*
12. Too Much Money, Right? Morris and Eddie are going to Super AdventureLand on their Chol Hamoed trip. They ask their friend Ezra if he wants to come with them, and he says he has to ask his mother. "My mother said we have other plans for today," he tells them. "Oh," they say knowingly. "Is it too much money?" Why was their question inappropriate? Is there any way Ezra could answer truthfully without disclosing information that he doesn't wish to disclose?	SCENARIO 12 ANSWERS AND THOUGHTS *Asking people about money is bound to make them feel uncomfortable, especially when there's a good chance they don't have it.*

13. Please Don't Flip My Tie

Danny's mother buys him a new tie. Danny likes the tie a lot – until he flips it over and looks at the tag. "I can't wear a polyester tie!" he says. "The guys are going to make fun of me!"

"How can they possibly know?" his mother wonders. "It's a beautiful tie – you can't tell that it's not silk."

"But what if they decide to flip my tie and check?" Danny asks.

"I can't believe kids would do that," his mother says confidently.

"But if you're worried, you can just cut out the tag."

"Then they'll for sure know it's polyester," Danny insists. "Trust me, I can't wear this tie."

Is Danny being overly anxious? Is there anything wrong with a polyester tie? Why do some people need to know what other people's tags say (whether the tags say the brand name, price, fabric content, etc.)?

SCENARIO 13 ANSWERS AND THOUGHTS

Unfortunately, kids don't always respect other people's personal space and boundaries. There's nothing wrong with wearing a polyester tie, but it's also understandable that Danny wouldn't want to advertise what his tie is made out of. But some people feel better about themselves when they expose the perceived weak points of others.

14. The Favor of Not Flaunting

"Uh, I can't study Monday night," says Ralph. "It's not going to work for me. I'm really sorry, Sammy."

Levi looks up at his brother Ralph, who is just hanging up the phone. "Why didn't you tell your friend that we go out to eat in a restaurant with Grandma & Grandpa every week?" he asks.

"I don't know if Sammy's family is able to go out to eat ever," Ralph says. "Why mention it?"

Would Sammy care if he knew that Ralph ate out with his grandparents every week?

How would Ralph's relationship with Sammy be different if Ralph would come into class every week and chat about what he ordered the night before at this week's fancy restaurant? If people would talk less about the things they have that other people might not have, what favor would they be doing?

SCENARIO 14 ANSWERS AND THOUGHTS

Sammy might not care if he knew that Ralph ate out with his grandparents. But if he was constantly hearing about Ralph's restaurant choices, he might eventually start to feel that it's normal and necessary to eat out in restaurants. Conspicuous consumption alters the norms of society and raises people's standards of what's necessary to be happy. Inconspicuous consumption allows you to enjoy what you have without making others feel that they have to have it too.

15. Social Responsibility: Your Scenario

Choosing one of the four values listed below, think of a scenario (real or imagined) that would demonstrate the value. The scenario can highlight the value in either a positive or a negative manner.

1. **Positive peer pressure**
2. **Avoiding conspicuous consumption**
3. **Discretion and privacy**
4. **What you have is not what you are**

UNIT 6

BECOMING A SMART CONSUMER

Unit 6

Becoming a Smart Consumer

1. *To recognize that keeping track of consumption is the first step in becoming a smart consumer.*
2. *To appreciate the value of even small amounts of money.*
3. *To understand that both costs and savings multiply.*
4. *To learn about the ripple effect of smart spending decisions: if you spend less on the things that are less important, you'll have more to spend on the things that are more important.*
5. *To gain familiarity with the concept of unit cost and learn to break down a product into its component prices.*
6. *To acquire good shopping skills and learn to make the most of your money.*

Materials:

- 2 lesson plans for teacher
- Workbook pages:
  - **A Tale of 10 Coffees**
  - **Have Your Cake – And Pay for it, Too!**
  - **Shop Like a Pro**

Lesson 1: Every Penny Counts

Goal: To recognize that keeping track of consumption is the first step in becoming a smart consumer.

Instructions

Mesila has found that lack of spending awareness is a major factor in financial instability. People often have no idea how much they are spending, and on what – and then they wonder why they never seem to have enough money. Lack of spending awareness is most pronounced in the small purchases; people generally know how much their mortgage, tuition, and car insurance cost, but are typically shocked to discover how much money disappears on the little things: parking fees, thingamajigs, newspapers... and, of course, a good cup of coffee. Some of these expenditures are necessary, but many of them can be greatly minimized just by being aware of what is being spent.

In the lesson that follows, we present ten different cost options for a very similar product: a cup of coffee. The price per cup ranges from $0.10 to $6.25, and the difference between buying the $0.10 cup every day and buying the $6.25 cup every day adds up to thousands of dollars a year – and that's just for one cup a day.

Although this lesson is geared to students who do not (or should not) drink coffee, we have deliberately chosen this example before they form habits that are hard to break later.

Workbook: A Tale of Ten Coffees

Instructions

The purpose of this exercise is not to practice mathematical skills, but rather to emphasize in a very real way how small savings add up very quickly, and how people can save themselves lots of money by paying attention to their lifestyle habits and making minor adjustments.

This should be completed as a class activity, with a lighthearted, fun tone. You may have to help the students calculate the answers to the questions, or even tell them the answers if you feel that the mathematics is difficult or distracting from the main message.

Has this ever happened to you? You take out your wallet, sure that it's going to be full – **but it's empty!** *Where did all the money go?* you wonder. Keeping track of the small stuff is challenging, but it can do wonders for your finances. Trivial purchases add up: 50 cents here, $2 here, and before you know it, that money from your grandparents is gone.

This happens to adults, too. **Let's take a look at one of the ways that people's pocket change disappears.**

Coffee Type	Price per Cup	Price per Week (1 cup a day)	Price per Year (1 cup a day)	Price per Year (3 coffee drinkers in the house, 1 coffee a day each)
1. Homemade, Folgers instant	$0.10	$0.70	$36.50	
2. Homemade, Taster's Choice instant	$0.16	$1.12	$58.40	
3. Homemade, Taster's Choice singles	$0.25	$1.75	$91.25	
4. Homemade, brewed in a Keurig with individual packages	$0.50	$3.50	$182.50	
5. Homemade, iced coffee	$0.60	$4.20	$219	
6. Convenience store, regular coffee	$1.75	$12.25	$638.75	
7. Coffee shop, iced coffee	$1.99	$13.93	$726.35	
8. Coffee shop, latte or cappucino	$3.49	$24.43	$1273.85	
9. Coffee shop, frappucino	$3.99	$27.93	$1,456.35	
10. Restaurant, gourmet	$6.25	$43.75	$2,281.25	

41

Answers to Questions:

1. The answers are calculated by multiplying each number in the fourth column by three:

$109.50
$175.20
$273.75
$547.50
$657.00
$1914.00
$2179.05
$3821.55
$4369.05
$6843.75

2. The answer is calculated by determining the difference between a store-bought frappucino ($3.99) and a homemade Keurig brewed coffee ($0.50):

   $3.99 – $0.50 = $3.49

3. The answer is calculated by multiplying the cost of a Folgers instant coffee by seven days a week ($0.10 x 7) and adding the cost of a latte multiplied by five days a week ($3.49 x 5).

   ($0.10 x 7) + ($3.49 x 5) = $18.15

4. The answer is calculated in two steps:

   a. Calculating the profit per cup, which is the difference between the amount Chani and Suri charged for the coffee and the amount it cost them to make it at home:

      $1.75 - $0.60 = $1.15

   b. Multiplying the profit per cup by the number of cups:

      $1.15 x 100 = $115

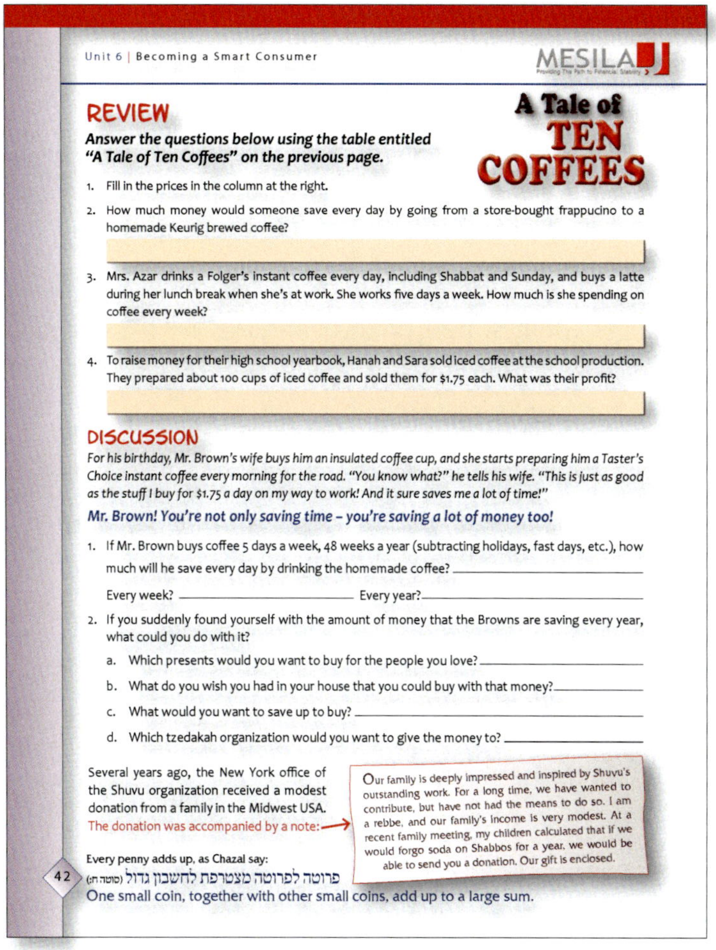

Unit 6 | Becoming a Smart Consumer

MESILA

A Tale of TEN COFFEES

REVIEW

Answer the questions below using the table entitled "A Tale of Ten Coffees" on the previous page.

1. Fill in the prices in the column at the right.
2. How much money would someone save every day by going from a store-bought frappucino to a homemade Keurig brewed coffee?
3. Mrs. Azar drinks a Folger's instant coffee every day, including Shabbat and Sunday, and buys a latte during her lunch break when she's at work. She works five days a week. How much is she spending on coffee every week?
4. To raise money for their high school yearbook, Hanah and Sara sold iced coffee at the school production. They prepared about 100 cups of iced coffee and sold them for $1.75 each. What was their profit?

DISCUSSION

For his birthday, Mr. Brown's wife buys him an insulated coffee cup, and she starts preparing him a Taster's Choice instant coffee every morning for the road. "You know what?" he tells his wife. "This is just as good as the stuff I buy for $1.75 a day on my way to work! And it sure saves me a lot of time!"

Mr. Brown! You're not only saving time – you're saving a lot of money too!

1. If Mr. Brown buys coffee 5 days a week, 48 weeks a year (subtracting holidays, fast days, etc.), how much will he save every day by drinking the homemade coffee? ______
   Every week? ______ Every year? ______
2. If you suddenly found yourself with the amount of money that the Browns are saving every year, what could you do with it?
   a. Which presents would you want to buy for the people you love? ______
   b. What do you wish you had in your house that you could buy with that money? ______
   c. What would you want to save up to buy? ______
   d. Which tzedakah organization would you want to give the money to? ______

Several years ago, the New York office of the Shuvu organization received a modest donation from a family in the Midwest USA. The donation was accompanied by a note:

Our family is deeply impressed and inspired by Shuvu's outstanding work. For a long time, we have wanted to contribute, but have not had the means to do so. I am a rebbe, and our family's income is very modest. At a recent family meeting, my children calculated that if we would forgo soda on Shabbos for a year, we would be able to send you a donation. Our gift is enclosed.

Every penny adds up, as Chazal say:

פרוטה לפרוטה מצטרפת לחשבון גדול (סוטה ח)

One small coin, together with other small coins, add up to a large sum.

42

Discussion Answers:

The first answer is calculated by determining the difference between a $1.75 store coffee and a $0.16 Taster's Choice instant coffee:

$1.75 - $0.16 = $1.59

The second answer is calculated by multiplying the savings per day ($1.59) by 5 days a week:

$1.59 x 5 = $7.95

The third answer is calculated by multiplying the savings per week by 48:

$7.95 x 48 = $381.60

Workbook: Have Your Cake - And Pay for It, Too!

Goal

To introduce the concept of unit cost and discover how to determine the actual price of a product.

Instructions

In the first part of this exercise, we tell the amusing story of "Shmiel Schlemiel" and his adventures in trying to prepare his very first chocolate cake. When Shmiel goes shopping for the ingredients, he is shocked to discover that the total cost of all these ingredients is approximately the same as buying a readymade store-bought cake. What he doesn't realize, of course, is that the actual cost of the homemade cake is a fraction of the cost of his shopping list, simply because only a portion of each ingredient will be used.

In the assignment that follows the tale of Shmiel Schlemiel's adventures, students are asked to calculate the actual cost of preparing a recipe.

Unit 6 | Becoming a Smart Consumer

Understanding Unit Cost

HAVE YOUR CAKE - AND PAY FOR IT, TOO!

Shmiel Schlemiel, the new yeshiva cook, decides to bake his very first chocolate cake for the boys. He takes his chocolate cake recipe out of his brand-new recipe box and takes it to the store as a shopping list:

MAMA'S BEST CHOCOLATE CAKE
2 EGGS
2 CUPS SUGAR
½ CUP OIL
1 ½ TEASPOONS INSTANT COFFEE, DISSOLVED IN ¼ CUP HOT WATER
1 ¾ CUPS WATER
1 TEASPOON VANILLA EXTRACT
1 ¾ CUPS FLOUR
¾ CUP COCOA
2 TEASPOONS BAKING POWDER
1 TEASPOON BAKING SODA
DIRECTIONS: BAKE IN A 9X13 PAN AT 350° FOR 50-60 MINUTE

This is what his store receipt said:

KOSHERmart
Food you love.Food for life

A dozen eggs	$1.99
5 lb. sugar	$3.99
1/2 gallon oil	$6.49
1 jar instant coffee	$5.99
1 bottle vanilla extract	$3.19
5 lb. flour	$3.49
1 can cocoa	$3.89
1 container baking powder	$1.79
1 container baking soda	$1.49
TOTAL:	$32.31

TC# 0432 2121 1542 2401 9590
Laweway is back for Electronics, Toys, and Jewelry. 10/17/11-12/16/11
11/06/11 02:22:59

"What a ripoff!" Shmiel thinks.
"This cake is costing the Yeshiva $32!
I should have bought a fancy cream cake at the bakery down the block, for only $28!"

Shmiel, Shmiel, don't be such a Shlemiel!
This cake is not costing you $32!

43

Instructions

In the "Price It" assignment, we ask the students to break down a recipe into its component ingredients and their respective prices. This should be done in a way that is enjoyable for the class, and not a burdensome mathematical exercise. Encourage the students to choose simple recipes, rather than elaborate ones, and allow them to estimate the costs of ingredients for which they have trouble determining prices. They should feel free to ask a parent or older sibling for help; this does not have to be completed independently, since the point is to gain a financial lesson, not a mathematical one.

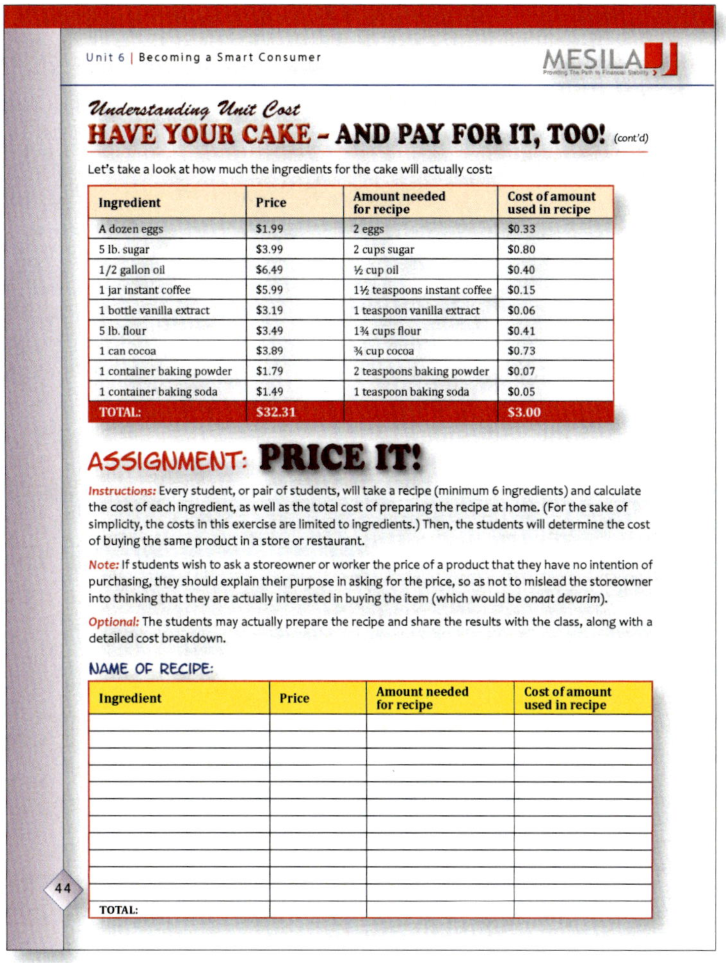

Unit 6 | Becoming a Smart Consumer

Understanding Unit Cost

HAVE YOUR CAKE – AND PAY FOR IT, TOO! *(cont'd)*

Let's take a look at how much the ingredients for the cake will actually cost:

Ingredient	Price	Amount needed for recipe	Cost of amount used in recipe
A dozen eggs	$1.99	2 eggs	$0.33
5 lb. sugar	$3.99	2 cups sugar	$0.80
1/2 gallon oil	$6.49	½ cup oil	$0.40
1 jar instant coffee	$5.99	1½ teaspoons instant coffee	$0.15
1 bottle vanilla extract	$3.19	1 teaspoon vanilla extract	$0.06
5 lb. flour	$3.49	1¾ cups flour	$0.41
1 can cocoa	$3.89	¾ cup cocoa	$0.73
1 container baking powder	$1.79	2 teaspoons baking powder	$0.07
1 container baking soda	$1.49	1 teaspoon baking soda	$0.05
TOTAL:	$32.31		$3.00

ASSIGNMENT: PRICE IT!

Instructions: Every student, or pair of students, will take a recipe (minimum 6 ingredients) and calculate the cost of each ingredient, as well as the total cost of preparing the recipe at home. (For the sake of simplicity, the costs in this exercise are limited to ingredients.) Then, the students will determine the cost of buying the same product in a store or restaurant.

Note: If students wish to ask a storeowner or worker the price of a product that they have no intention of purchasing, they should explain their purpose in asking for the price, so as not to mislead the storeowner into thinking that they are actually interested in buying the item (which would be *onaat devarim*).

Optional: The students may actually prepare the recipe and share the results with the class, along with a detailed cost breakdown.

NAME OF RECIPE:

Ingredient	Price	Amount needed for recipe	Cost of amount used in recipe
TOTAL:			

44

Lesson 2: Shop Like a Pro

Goal

To acquaint students with some basic techniques for minimizing costs and maximizing value.

Instructions

This lesson should begin with a review of the "Price it!" assignment that was given out at the end of the previous class. This review can be conducted in two ways:

1. **Informal:** By having the students sample each other's culinary experiments while analyzing and commenting on the cost breakdown of each.
2. **Formal:** By choosing several students to present the cost breakdown of their respective recipes, and then having all of the students hand in their assignments to be graded by the teacher.

The next part of the lesson will be a discussion of effective shopping techniques, based on the tips and examples presented in **workpage #3: Shop Like a Pro**. The tips and examples in this workpage focus exclusively on keeping costs down, which is certainly the major consideration in smart spending decisions. However, once the students have gained an appreciation for cost savings, you may want to familiarize them with other factors that might legitimately influence spending decisions. These include:

1. **Quality/Taste/Performance:** When a particular company or product has proven itself to be superior to its competitors, one might choose to spend the extra money.
2. **Economy of scale:** Bulk items come with a higher price tag, but actually cost less per unit.
3. **Convenience:** At times, it might be worthwhile to spend more money to save time and/or energy. (Refer to the time-energy-money triangle in Unit 4, Budgeting.)
4. **Hidden or peripheral costs:** A cheaper product may wind up costing more, once you take all the hidden costs into account. Examples:
   a. Travel costs: gas, parking, tolls
   b. Repairs and replacement of cheap items that break
   c. Low-cost appliances that are not energy efficient and require more electricity to run
5. **Customer service:** It may be worth paying more for a product that comes with good service (e.g., warrantee, good return/exchange policy).
6. **Values:** Money is not the most important thing in the world. People pay more for things that matter to them. Examples:
   a. Kosher food (e.g., Chalav Yisrael milk)
   b. Healthier products (e.g., whole wheat bread)
   c. Patronizing stores owned by members of the community, or stores that respect your religious sensitivities.

Depending on the maturity level of your class, you may decide to introduce these factors, or alternatively, to focus exclusively on costly vs. inexpensive prices.

Workbook: Shop Like a Pro

SHOP LIKE A PRO!

Here are some tips for keeping costs down and making the most of your money:

SALE 1

If you're planning to buy a few items, make a shopping list. And stick to it!

Example: Harry went to the store planning to buy a pen and a notebook for school. When he spotted the new stickers on sale, he took a few packages off the shelf. When he got home, he discovered that he had spent twice as much as he had planned, on stuff that he didn't really want!

SALE 2

Pay attention to the various sizes available of the item you want. Larger packages are generally cheaper per item (assuming that you need the larger quantity).

Example: Max is buying cups for the class siyum. He can buy two packages of 12 cups for 99 cents each, or one package of 25 for $1.49.

SALE 3

Price the item you want in different stores. (You can just call them; you don't even have to go in.)

Example: Michael saved up his birthday money and Chanukah money until he had enough for the type of camera he wanted. He called six different stores and found that there was a range of $37 between the cheapest and the most expensive price – for the same camera model.

SALE 4

Generally, smaller stores (such as groceries) charge more than larger stores (such as supermarkets).

Example: Albert's mother sent him to buy a container of ice cream. At the corner grocery, it was priced at $8.49. At the supermarket it cost $5.69.

SALE 5

Stores stock basic items at the back of the store, and non-essential items in the front – or at the checkout counter – to get you to buy things you don't really need.

Example: Benny ran over to the store to pick up milk, bread, and eggs. Somehow, by the time he left the store, his bags also contained some chocolate bars and chewing gum that he had passed along the way.

SALE 6

A sale isn't a bargain unless you really need it.

Example: Avi was on line buying himself an ices for $1.75. The cashier told him, "If you buy five of those, they're on special for $5."
"But I only need one," Avi answered – and saved himself $3.25.

SALE 7

Don't shop when you're hungry.

Example: Dave stopped at a convenience store on his way home from yeshiva to buy some scotch tape. He was so famished, that when he spotted a bag of barbecue potato chips, he just picked it off the shelf and bought it. He didn't have much of an appetite for his mother's delicious supper when he came home.

SALE 8

Bring approximately the amount of money that you need, and not much more.

Example: Seymour is on a class trip with his friends. He wanted to bring along money to buy a cold drink, but he only had a $20 bill. After he bought his drink, and was left with a pocket full of change, he wandered into the souvenir shop and bought some gifts for his family. When he came home, he started wondering what in the world his parents would do with the stuffed lizard and "I ♥ NY" paperweight he had brought them.

SALE 9

If you buy the wrong thing, return or exchange it. Right away.

Example: After Joseph went off to yeshiva in Eretz Yisrael, his mother found a line-up of pants and jackets hanging in his closet, all with the tags still on. He had picked them up during his pre-flight shopping, but they turned out to be too snug on him... "Too bad it's too late to return this stuff," his mother mourned. "It's worth a fortune."

SALE 10

Count your change, and check your receipt for mistakes.

Example: Moshe bought a $2 flashlight for camp and paid with a $10 bill. It's a good thing he noticed that the cashier had given him four $1 bills instead of three $1 bills and one $5 bill. When he looked at his receipt, he saw that he had been charged $6 for the flashlight instead of $2.

Activity

Workbook: Shop Like a Pro - "Madlibs"

Below are two short stories about kids going shopping for camp, one of whom is following the "Shop Like a Pro" tips and one of whom is not. Before reading the story to the class, ask the students to provide the missing parts of speech indicated in the stories, and write down each word in its proper place in the story. (The funnier and zanier the words they come up with, the more entertaining the results will be.)

Note: The students should not have these workbook pages open in front of them during the activity.

When you have finished filling in all the missing words, read the stories back to the class – for a hilarious, but educational conclusion to this unit.

Alternatively, you can pair the students up, and give out the "Madlib" sheet to one student in each pair, with the other providing the missing words.

This activity is a good review of the shopping tips in the preceding workbook pages, and is an opportunity to highlight good and bad shopping habits.

After enjoying the Madlib activity with the class, have the students open their workbooks and fill in the missing words in a way that makes sense and reinforces the smart shopping habits imparted in this unit.

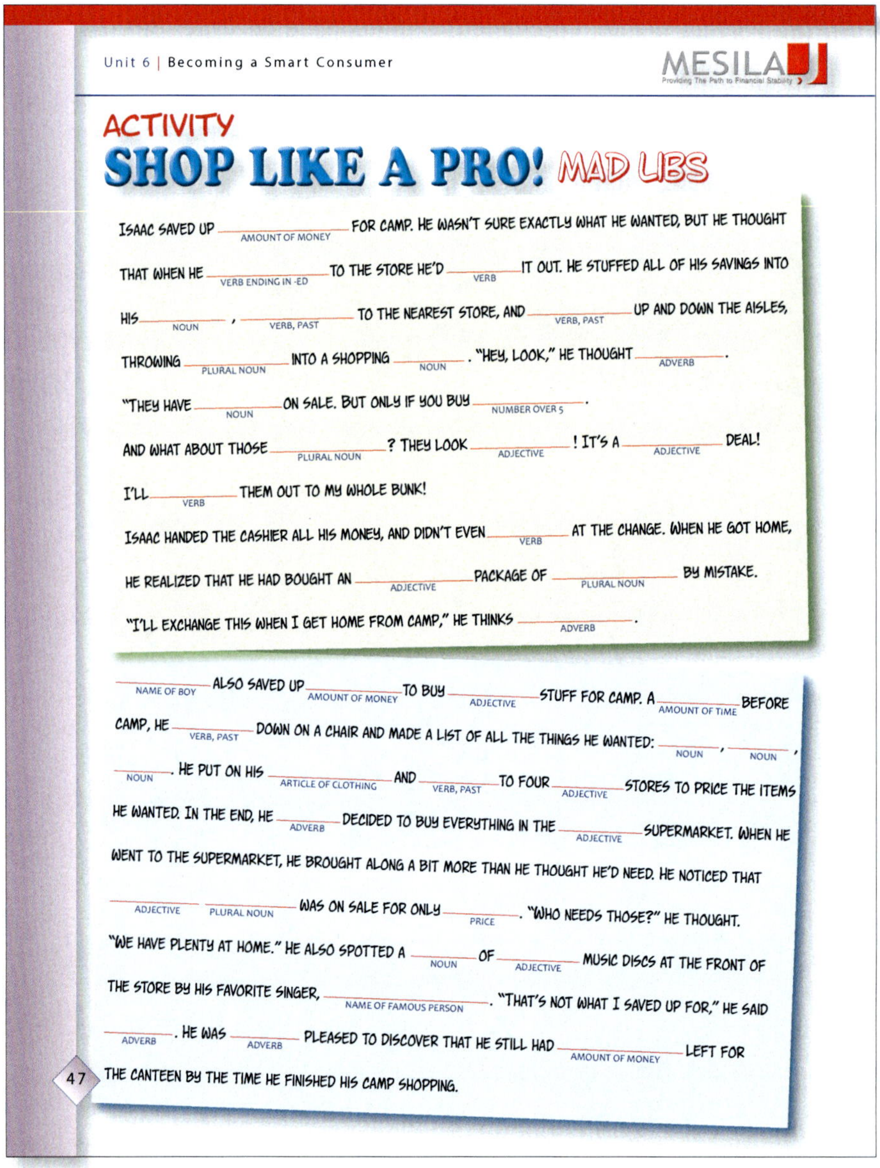

Unit 6 | Becoming a Smart Consumer

ACTIVITY

SHOP LIKE A PRO! MAD LIBS

ISAAC SAVED UP ________ (AMOUNT OF MONEY) FOR CAMP. HE WASN'T SURE EXACTLY WHAT HE WANTED, BUT HE THOUGHT THAT WHEN HE ________ (VERB ENDING IN -ED) TO THE STORE HE'D ________ (VERB) IT OUT. HE STUFFED ALL OF HIS SAVINGS INTO HIS ________ (NOUN), ________ (VERB, PAST) TO THE NEAREST STORE, AND ________ (VERB, PAST) UP AND DOWN THE AISLES, THROWING ________ (PLURAL NOUN) INTO A SHOPPING ________ (NOUN). "HEY, LOOK," HE THOUGHT ________ (ADVERB). "THEY HAVE ________ (NOUN) ON SALE. BUT ONLY IF YOU BUY ________ (NUMBER OVER 5). AND WHAT ABOUT THOSE ________ (PLURAL NOUN)? THEY LOOK ________ (ADJECTIVE)! IT'S A ________ (ADJECTIVE) DEAL! I'LL ________ (VERB) THEM OUT TO MY WHOLE BUNK! ISAAC HANDED THE CASHIER ALL HIS MONEY, AND DIDN'T EVEN ________ (VERB) AT THE CHANGE. WHEN HE GOT HOME, HE REALIZED THAT HE HAD BOUGHT AN ________ (ADJECTIVE) PACKAGE OF ________ (PLURAL NOUN) BY MISTAKE. "I'LL EXCHANGE THIS WHEN I GET HOME FROM CAMP," HE THINKS ________ (ADVERB).

________ (NAME OF BOY) ALSO SAVED UP ________ (AMOUNT OF MONEY) TO BUY ________ (ADJECTIVE) STUFF FOR CAMP. A ________ (AMOUNT OF TIME) BEFORE CAMP, HE ________ (VERB, PAST) DOWN ON A CHAIR AND MADE A LIST OF ALL THE THINGS HE WANTED: ________ (NOUN), ________ (NOUN), ________ (NOUN). HE PUT ON HIS ________ (ARTICLE OF CLOTHING) AND ________ (VERB, PAST) TO FOUR ________ (ADJECTIVE) STORES TO PRICE THE ITEMS HE WANTED. IN THE END, HE ________ (ADVERB) DECIDED TO BUY EVERYTHING IN THE ________ (ADJECTIVE) SUPERMARKET. WHEN HE WENT TO THE SUPERMARKET, HE BROUGHT ALONG A BIT MORE THAN HE THOUGHT HE'D NEED. HE NOTICED THAT ________ (ADJECTIVE) ________ (PLURAL NOUN) WAS ON SALE FOR ONLY ________ (PRICE). "WHO NEEDS THOSE?" HE THOUGHT. "WE HAVE PLENTY AT HOME." HE ALSO SPOTTED A ________ (NOUN) OF ________ (ADJECTIVE) MUSIC DISCS AT THE FRONT OF THE STORE BY HIS FAVORITE SINGER, ________ (NAME OF FAMOUS PERSON). "THAT'S NOT WHAT I SAVED UP FOR," HE SAID ________ (ADVERB). HE WAS ________ (ADVERB) PLEASED TO DISCOVER THAT HE STILL HAD ________ (AMOUNT OF MONEY) LEFT FOR THE CANTEEN BY THE TIME HE FINISHED HIS CAMP SHOPPING.

47

UNIT 7

RESPECTING PROPERTY

Unit 7

Respecting Property *Yours, Ours & Theirs*

Educational goals

1. *To explain the importance of boundaries between a person's own property, the property of others, and communal property.*
2. *To impart the basic halachot of integrity as they apply to other people's money and property.*
3. *To learn to apply the halachot integrity to common real-life situations.*
4. *To develop sensitivity and respect for communal property.*

Materials

- 1 lesson plan for teacher
- Workbook pages:
  - **Basic halachot of integrity**
  - **Integrity exercise**
- Activity: Class Fair

To the teacher

The purpose of this unit is to convey the oft-forgotten value of respecting property. Because the nature of this topic is highly individual, depending on the specific issues in a particular classroom and community, we leave it to teachers to expand the material in a way that they deem most relevant for their audience. We have included basic principles and applications, which may be adjusted and amplified as per the teacher's discretion.

Workbook: Yours, Ours & Theirs

Goal

To familiarize students with practical halachot relating to property.

Instructions

This worksheet contains very basic halachot along with sources. No source is given for the first, seventh, and ninth halachot, because those are basic Torah principles that are self-evident and need no expansion. When imparting these halachot, the emphasis should be on how integral these concepts are: they are not subject to any dispute or flexibility.

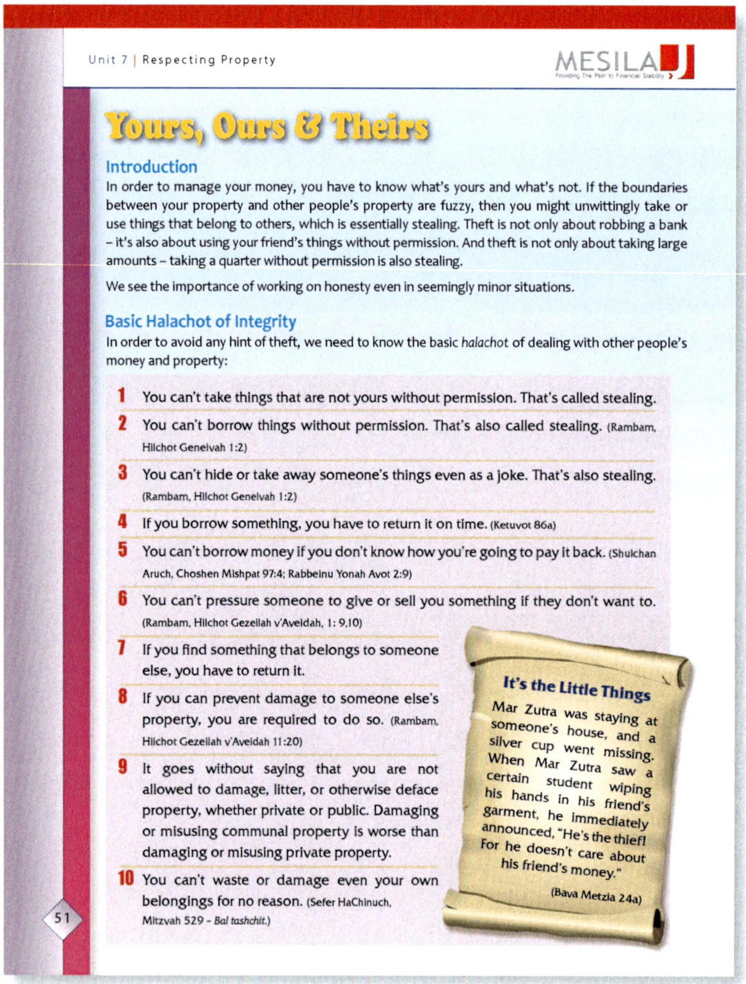

Unit 7 | Respecting Property

MESILA

Yours, Ours & Theirs

Introduction

In order to manage your money, you have to know what's yours and what's not. If the boundaries between your property and other people's property are fuzzy, then you might unwittingly take or use things that belong to others, which is essentially stealing. Theft is not only about robbing a bank – it's also about using your friend's things without permission. And theft is not only about taking large amounts – taking a quarter without permission is also stealing.

We see the importance of working on honesty even in seemingly minor situations.

Basic Halachot of Integrity

In order to avoid any hint of theft, we need to know the basic *halachot* of dealing with other people's money and property:

1. You can't take things that are not yours without permission. That's called stealing.
2. You can't borrow things without permission. That's also called stealing. (Rambam, Hilchot Geneivah 1:2)
3. You can't hide or take away someone's things even as a joke. That's also stealing. (Rambam, Hilchot Geneivah 1:2)
4. If you borrow something, you have to return it on time. (Ketuvot 86a)
5. You can't borrow money if you don't know how you're going to pay it back. (Shulchan Aruch, Choshen Mishpat 97:4; Rabbeinu Yonah Avot 2:9)
6. You can't pressure someone to give or sell you something if they don't want to. (Rambam, Hilchot Gezeilah v'Aveidah, 1: 9,10)
7. If you find something that belongs to someone else, you have to return it.
8. If you can prevent damage to someone else's property, you are required to do so. (Rambam, Hilchot Gezeilah v'Aveidah 11:20)
9. It goes without saying that you are not allowed to damage, litter, or otherwise deface property, whether private or public. Damaging or misusing communal property is worse than damaging or misusing private property.
10. You can't waste or damage even your own belongings for no reason. (Sefer HaChinuch, Mitzvah 529 - *Bal tashchit.*)

It's the Little Things

Mar Zutra was staying at someone's house, and a silver cup went missing. When Mar Zutra saw a certain student wiping his hands in his friend's garment, he immediately announced, "He's the thief! For he doesn't care about his friend's money."

(Bava Metzia 24a)

51

Workbook: Yours, Ours & Theirs

Goal

To practice applying the halachot of integrity in a hands-on way.

Instructions

Each of the 17 scenarios presented corresponds to one (or more) of the 10 halachot enumerated in the previous worksheet. Feel free to add scenarios or have the students suggest their own.

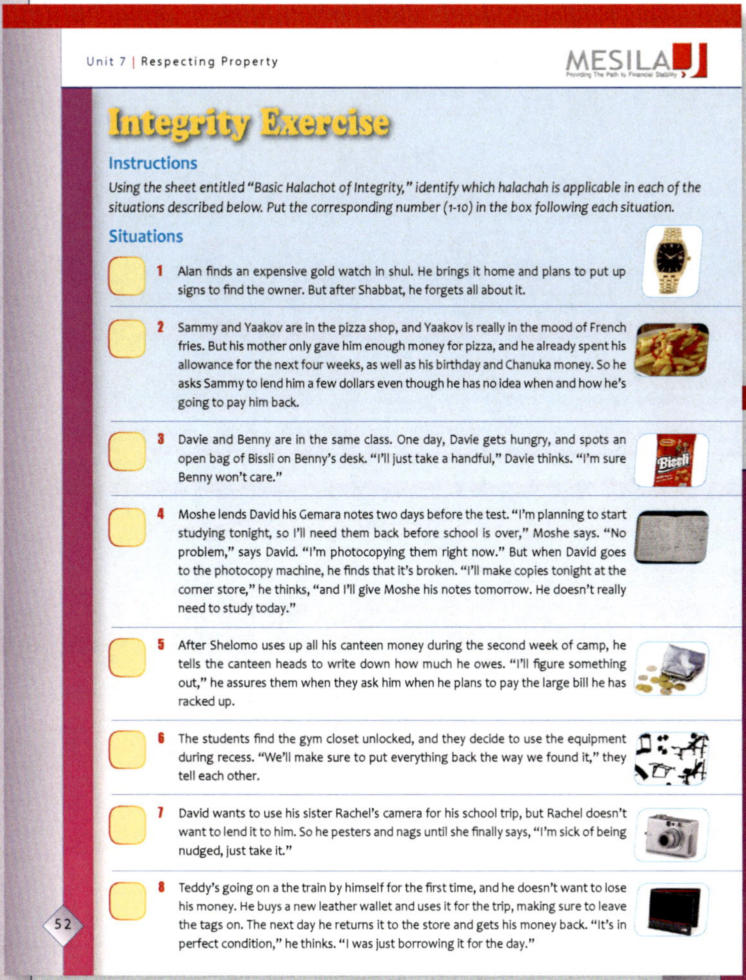
Unit 7 | Respecting Property

MESILA

Integrity Exercise

Instructions

Using the sheet entitled "Basic Halachot of Integrity," identify which halachah is applicable in each of the situations described below. Put the corresponding number (1-10) in the box following each situation.

Situations

1 Alan finds an expensive gold watch in shul. He brings it home and plans to put up signs to find the owner. But after Shabbat, he forgets all about it.

2 Sammy and Yaakov are in the pizza shop, and Yaakov is really in the mood of French fries. But his mother only gave him enough money for pizza, and he already spent his allowance for the next four weeks, as well as his birthday and Chanuka money. So he asks Sammy to lend him a few dollars even though he has no idea when and how he's going to pay him back.

3 Davie and Benny are in the same class. One day, Davie gets hungry, and spots an open bag of Bissli on Benny's desk. "I'll just take a handful," Davie thinks. "I'm sure Benny won't care."

4 Moshe lends David his Gemara notes two days before the test. "I'm planning to start studying tonight, so I'll need them back before school is over," Moshe says. "No problem," says David. "I'm photocopying them right now." But when David goes to the photocopy machine, he finds that it's broken. "I'll make copies tonight at the corner store," he thinks, "and I'll give Moshe his notes tomorrow. He doesn't really need to study today."

5 After Shelomo uses up all his canteen money during the second week of camp, he tells the canteen heads to write down how much he owes. "I'll figure something out," he assures them when they ask him when he plans to pay the large bill he has racked up.

6 The students find the gym closet unlocked, and they decide to use the equipment during recess. "We'll make sure to put everything back the way we found it," they tell each other.

7 David wants to use his sister Rachel's camera for his school trip, but Rachel doesn't want to lend it to him. So he pesters and nags until she finally says, "I'm sick of being nudged, just take it."

8 Teddy's going on a the train by himself for the first time, and he doesn't want to lose his money. He buys a new leather wallet and uses it for the trip, making sure to leave the tags on. The next day he returns it to the store and gets his money back. "It's in perfect condition," he thinks. "I was just borrowing it for the day."

52

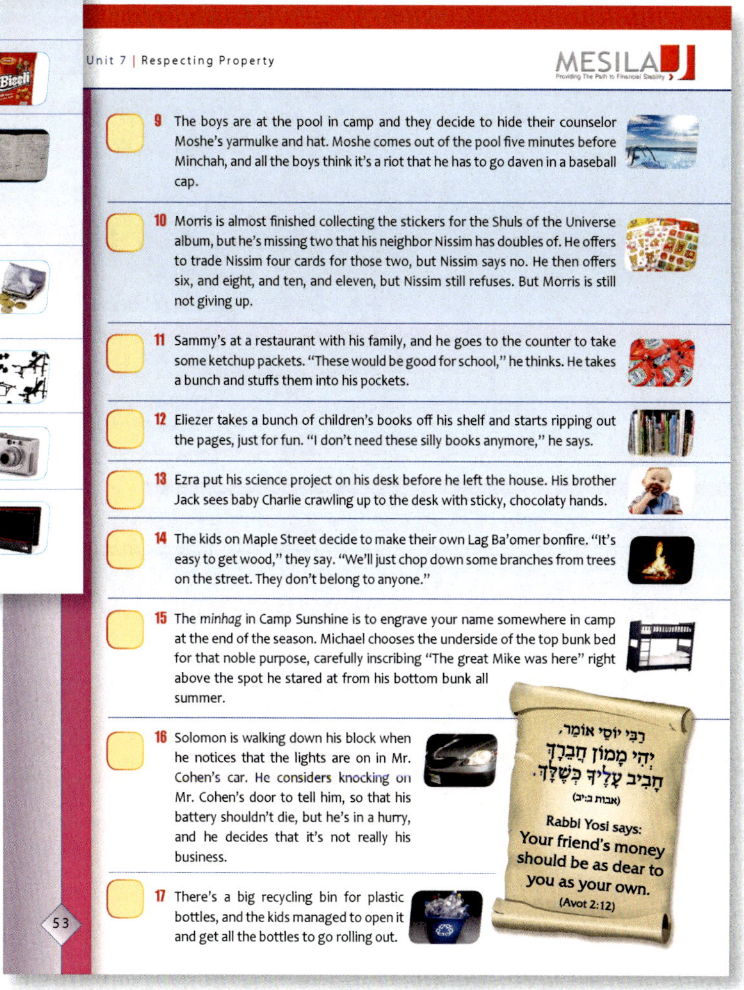
Unit 7 | Respecting Property

MESILA

9 The boys are at the pool in camp and they decide to hide their counselor Moshe's yarmulke and hat. Moshe comes out of the pool five minutes before Minchah, and all the boys think it's a riot that he has to go daven in a baseball cap.

10 Morris is almost finished collecting the stickers for the Shuls of the Universe album, but he's missing two that his neighbor Nissim has doubles of. He offers to trade Nissim four cards for those two, but Nissim says no. He then offers six, and eight, and ten, and eleven, but Nissim still refuses. But Morris is still not giving up.

11 Sammy's at a restaurant with his family, and he goes to the counter to take some ketchup packets. "These would be good for school," he thinks. He takes a bunch and stuffs them into his pockets.

12 Eliezer takes a bunch of children's books off his shelf and starts ripping out the pages, just for fun. "I don't need these silly books anymore," he says.

13 Ezra put his science project on his desk before he left the house. His brother Jack sees baby Charlie crawling up to the desk with sticky, chocolaty hands.

14 The kids on Maple Street decide to make their own Lag Ba'omer bonfire. "It's easy to get wood," they say. "We'll just chop down some branches from trees on the street. They don't belong to anyone."

15 The *minhag* in Camp Sunshine is to engrave your name somewhere in camp at the end of the season. Michael chooses the underside of the top bunk bed for that noble purpose, carefully inscribing "The great Mike was here" right above the spot he stared at from his bottom bunk all summer.

16 Solomon is walking down his block when he notices that the lights are on in Mr. Cohen's car. He considers knocking on Mr. Cohen's door to tell him, so that his battery shouldn't die, but he's in a hurry, and he decides that it's not really his business.

17 There's a big recycling bin for plastic bottles, and the kids managed to open it and get all the bottles to go rolling out.

רבי יוסי אומר, יהי ממון חברך חביב עליך כשלך. (אבות ב:יב)

Rabbi Yosi says: Your friend's money should be as dear to you as your own. (Avot 2:12)

53

Workbook: Class Fair:
Respecting Property - Yours, Ours & Theirs

Respecting Property
Yours, Ours & Theirs

Objective

To visually depict areas in which respect for property needs strengthening.

Rationale

Often, people are not sufficiently mindful of their responsibility towards property, whether their own, someone else's, or the community's. The root causes of this behavior can be one of the following factors, or a combination:

- Carelessness
- Lack of integrity
- Lack of awareness or knowledge

Instructions

Every student, pair, or group will identify a particular area in which respect for property needs strengthening, and will design a visual exhibit illustrating the problematic behavior and depicting halachically acceptable alternatives.

The exhibit should demonstrate creativity and knowledge, and should have a practical message for its viewers.

Possible Topics

- Respect for shuls, yeshivot, and schools
- Wasteful or destructive behavior
- Respect for parents' money and property
- Respect for friends' money and property
- Misusing public property (parks, greenery, signs, etc.)
- Integrity with money
- Subtle forms of theft or dishonesty
- Jokes & pranks
- Responsible borrowing
- Returning lost objects

This can also be done as a class project for creating community awareness, or as a class newspaper.

UNIT 8

ADVERTISING

Unit 8
Advertising

Educational goals

1. *To demonstrate how advertisers create need and get people to part with their money.*
2. *To familiarize students with commonly used advertising techniques.*
3. *To help students understand that advertisers do not have their best interests in mind.*
4. *To cultivate healthy resistance and suspicion on the part of students towards advertisements, thus enabling them to withstand the enticements of the advertising industry.*

Materials

- 1 lesson plan for teacher
- PowerPoint presentation: **Hurry! Supplies are Limited!**
  How Advertisers Get You to Do What They Want
- Workbook pages:
  - **How Advertisers Play With Your Mind**
- Activity

To the teacher

Introduction

Advertising is a mega-billion dollar industry – and growing. Its entire purpose is to get people to buy things that they otherwise would not. One of the primary functions of advertising is to create needs and wants that never existed, in order to drive sales. (This concept is discussed further in Unit 3: Kids' Needs & Wants.)

Children are especially vulnerable to advertising because they lack the critical thinking faculties and cognitive defenses to understand what lies behind an innocent-looking advertisement. They do not realize that advertisers are trying to make money at their expense, and they naively swallow exhortations to buy, thinking that the advertisers truly have their best interests in mind.

Kids today have more access to money that in earlier times, but they still lack the healthy resistance that adults typically develop towards advertising strategies (although many adults never do develop enough resistance).

Worse, advertising appeals to people's senses and tries to create appetites where none existed. We as Torah educators are trying to imbue our students with self-control and self-discipline, and to discourage them from automatically giving in to their desires. Advertisers, on the other hand, actively encourage hedonism and excess. Unfortunately, this is often true of Jewish advertising as well.

It is therefore incumbent upon us to arm our students with tools to intelligently decipher the advertisements that surround them, and help them develop healthy immunity against these powerfully persuasive messages.

PowerPoint Presentation

Hurry! Supplies are Limited!

HOW ADVERTISERS GET YOU TO DO WHAT THEY WANT

Instructions

This PowerPoint presentation, developed by Mesila, visually depicts how advertisers play with people's minds and convince them to part with their money. The presentation opens with a general description of how advertisers create need, and then goes on to highlight specific techniques that are commonly used by advertisers. Understanding these techniques will empower students to resist them and immediately spot the psychological ploys being utilized in the advertisements they view.

There are innumerable techniques used by advertisers; we have chosen approximately 20 of the more basic ones.

This PowerPoint can be shown to the class as a stand-alone presentation, but is best used when augmented with teacher input and class discussion. We recommend that teachers stop the presentation at regular intervals to insert their own comments and encourage student discussion.

It is also advisable for teachers to supplement the presentation with examples culled from current circulars or periodicals.

Workbook: How Advertisers Play With Your Mind

Goal

To utilize advertising strategies in order to better understand how advertisers convince consumers to buy.

Instructions

This worksheet is essentially a synopsis of the various advertising techniques presented in the accompanying PowerPoint. It can be used either as an introduction to the PowerPoint, or as a review. It will also be used as a student reference in the activity that follows.

Unit 8 | Advertising

MESILA
Providing The Path to Financial Stability

How Advertisers PLAY With Your Mind

Advertisers use many different techniques in order to get you to buy their product. Here are some of the common ways they play with your mind:

Are supplies really limited? Or is this just a way to get you to the store, quick?

1 Unsubstantiated or Unprovable Claims

Promises that sound good, But can't be proven.

"Lowest prices anywhere."
"You won't find another house like this."
"Best ketchup."
"For skin like peaches and cream, use MagnaLotion."

2 Unfinished Claims

Claims that sound good, but mean nothing because they are not finished. They use words like less, reduced, lower-priced, or faster, better, cleaner, more, etc.

"UltraClean gives y ou more." More what?
"You can be sure if it's Westinghouse." Sure of what?

3 Guarantees

Advertisers try to make you think they're guaranteeing something, but that's not necessarily the case.

"Best photos. Guaranteed."
"Guaranteed to last."

4 Weasel Words*

A weasel word is one that appears meaningful at first glance but actually means nothing.

"Leaves dishes virtually spotless." (Virtually makes you think that it's spotless. But they didn't say that the dishes are actually going to be spotless.)
"Helps control dandruff." (The claim is not "stops dandruff.")

5 Free Stuff

Everyone likes to get something for nothing. But if you're paying for their product, it's not a free gift.

6 Buy One – Get Something "Free"

"Buy a burger – get free fries."

* The expression "weasel word" is named for the weasel's habit of sucking out the inside of an egg, leaving it hollow but appearing intact. Weasel words, therefore, appear to be making a meaningful claim, but actually say nothing. Here are some commonly used weasel words: "helps"; "virtually"; "almost like"; "can be"; "up to"; "as much as"; "refreshes"; "comforts"; "tackles"; "fights"; "strengthens"; "the feel of"; "looks like."

57

How Advertisers PLAY With Your Mind Cont'd 1

7 Buy One – Get a Discount

You feel like you're getting something extra, but when you do the math, it's not as good as it sounds.

"Buy one – get 25% off the second."
"Buy three – get one free."

8 You Deserve It

Why do you deserve what they want you to buy? And if you deserve it, why should you pay for it?

"You deserve a new dining room set."

9 Follow the Crowd

People like to belong and be part of the crowd.

"Everyone's drinking it – why aren't you?"

10 Stand Out From the Crowd

People also like to stand out and feel unique.

"Be different – do it your own way."

11 Rhetorical Questions

Advertisers ask you questions, leading your mind to come up with the answer they want.

"Shouldn't your family be drinking Hawaiian Punch?"
"Plymouth – isn't that the kind of car America wants?"

12 Catchy Slogans

Nothing like a good jingle or catchy phrase to stick in your mind and create a connection to a product or company.

"Coke. It's the Real Thing."
"Got milk?"

13 It's Good for You

Advertisers try to convince you that their product is good for you so that you'll feel that buying their product is the right thing to do.

"For heart health, go with our twelve-grain bread."
"Joe's Gym. Just what the doctor ordered."

14 Snob Appeal

Advertisers want you to feel special and "upper class" if you have their product.

"For people with good taste."
"SuperCool shampoo: For those who are a cut above."

15 Plain Folks

Some advertisements try to give you a comfortable, down-to-earth feeling.

"For people like you and me."

How Advertisers PLAY With Your Mind Cont'd 2

16 Scientific Evidence

By quoting statistics and medical or other scientific research, companies convince you that their product is effective.

"Proven clinical results."
"Studies show that Royal Paper Towels are 25% more absorbent."
"The headache medicine doctors recommend most."

17 Celebrity Endorsement

Advertisers try to convince you that if a famous person has one, then you should too.

18 Brand Loyalty and Designer Labels

Designers labels make you think there's something special about a particular brand. Companies try to get you to develop a preference for their brand and a positive association with their logo and packaging. They want you to be their friends.

19 Tradition & Family Values

Companies want to convince you that they are more trustworthy and valuable because they have been around for a long time, and they try to give you a warm, homey, family-like feeling.

"Family owned and operated since 1956."
"Where tradition and quality meet."

20 Feel-Good Experience

Advertisers try to get you to associate a particular product with a thrilling or otherwise positive experience.

"It's the next best thing to being there."
"Everest Furniture Polish – for that rugged mountain clean."

Activity - How advertisers play with your mind

Goal

To have students review and implement advertising tools discussed by rating Coca Cola ads and devising an ad or series of ads for a popular food.

Instructions

Part One

In this activity students will discuss either in small groups,individually, or as a class discussion if these ads are effective in getting people to spend money they hadn't planned on spending.

Other local ads can be introduced by the teacher to enhance the discussion.

This activity has many possible variations, depending on the level of complexity with which you'd like to challenge your students. You may choose to require one or more of the following:

- Use of multiple advertising techniques
- A full advertising campaign
- Use of different media (print, periodicals, audio-visual, virtual, etc.)
- Corporate branding: company name, logo, and slogan

Unit 8 | Advertising

MESILA

Activity:

How Advertisers Play With Your Mind

Part One

Below is an array of Coke ads.

Which ads are more likely to make you spend money you hadn't planned on spending? Rate them in order of appeal and effectiveness.

Part Two

Do It Yourself!

Choose a popular food and create an advertisement or series of advertisements promoting this food. The advertisements can include text, visual, audio, or a combination. Use at least one advertising technique or marketing strategy on the "How Advertisers Play With Your Mind" worksheet. How many techniques can you use?

60

Made in United States
Orlando, FL
04 November 2026

90201126R00043